1866-1991

125th

ANNIVERSARY

Also by Patrick F. McManus

Kid Camping From Aaaaiii! to Zip
A Fine and Pleasant Misery
They Shoot Canoes, Don't They?
The Grasshopper Trap
Rubber Legs and White Tail-Hairs
Whatchagot Stew
The Night the Bear Ate Goombaw
Real Ponies Don't Go Oink!

NEVER
SNIFF
A
GIFT FISH

Patrick F. McManus

An Owl Book

Henry Holt and Company • **New York**

Published by Henry Holt and Company, Inc.,
115 West 18th Street, New York, New York 10011.
Published in Canada by Fitzhenry & Whiteside Limited,
195 Allstate Parkway, Markham, Ontario L3R 4T8.

Library of Congress Cataloging-in-Publication Data
McManus, Patrick F.
Never sniff a gift fish.
1. Hunting—Addresses, essays, lectures. 2. Fishing—
Addresses, essays, lectures. I. Title.
SK33.M43   1983   799'.02'07   83-147
ISBN 0-8050-0527-7
ISBN 0-8050-0031-3 (An Owl book: pbk.)

Henry Holt books are available at special discounts
for bulk purchases for sales promotions, premiums,
fund-raising, or educational use. Special editions
or book excerpts can also be created to specification.

For details contact:
Special Sales Director
Henry Holt and Company, Inc.
115 West 18th Street
New York, New York 10011

First published in hardcover by Holt, Rinehart and
Winston in 1983.

First Owl Book Edition—1984

Designer: Kate Nichols
Printed in the United States of America
20   19   18

All stories in this book originally appeared as follows: In *Field &
Stream:* "Blowing Smoke," "The Man Who Notices Things," "The
Short Happy Life of Francis Cucumber," "Well, Excuuuuse Me!,"
"The Mountain Car," "Never Sniff a Gift Fish," "Edgy Rider," "The
Fibricators," "The Family Camper's Dictionary," "The Big Match,"
and "The Elk Trappers"; in *Outdoor Life:* "Poof—No Eyebrows!," "I
Fish; Therefore, I Am," "Running on Empty," "The Cat and the Cat
Burglar," "The Christmas Hatchet," "The Kindest Cut of All,"
"Share and Share Alike," "Backseats I Have Known," "The
Hunters' Workout Guide," "Temporary Measures," and "The Bush
Pilots"; in *Audubon:* "Salami on Rye and Hold the Wild Gobo," and
"Two-Man-Tent Fever"(and *Reader's Digest*); in *Daiwa Fishing
Annual:* "'Fish Poles,' and Other Useful Terminology"; in *Scotch
Game Call Annual:* "The Arkansas Prank Hound"; in *Spokane
Magazine:* "The Night Grandma Shot Shorty"; and in *Johnson
Outboards Boating 1980:* "Strange Scenes and Eerie Events."

To Patricia

Contents

Never Sniff a Gift Fish

Blowing Smoke

Many people think that my reputation as a great outdoorsman is a product of inherent athletic ability. Nothing could be further from the truth, which is that I have been cursed since birth with an extraordinary lack of coordination.

For years my fly-casting technique was compared, rather banally I might add, to an old lady fighting off a bee with a broom handle. My canoe paddling raised shouts of alarm among onlookers, who assumed I was trying to repel an assault by a North American cousin of the Loch Ness monster. My attempts to pitch the family tent terrorized entire campgrounds. As for marksmanship, any game I happened to bring into camp was routinely examined by my disbelieving companions for powder burns. ("The man has stealth," they would say. "Who else could place the muzzle of a rifle to the head of a sleeping mule-deer buck? Who else could still miss?")

1

For years I suffered the ridicule of my fellow sportsmen over what they perceived to be my ineptitude. Then one day I happened to recall a lovable old college administrator I had once served time under, Dr. Milburn Snodgrass. That casual recollection was to advance outdoor sports by a hundred years.

Doc Snodgrass had taken up pipe smoking as a young man and turned it into a highly successful career, eventually rising to the position of dean. Obviously, his success was not due merely to pipe smoking. No, he was also the master of two facial expressions: thoughtful and bemused. Those were the total ingredients of his success. The man was dumb. It is my considered opinion that if intelligence were crankcase oil, his would not have wet the tip of the dipstick let alone reached the add-one-quart mark. But he was an excellent dean.

No matter what problem was brought before Doc Snodgrass, his response was to sit back and puff on his pipe, alternating between thoughtful and bemused expressions. The effect suggested that Doc was bemused by a problem so ridiculously simple and was giving thought to firing the nincompoop who dared bother him with it. The problem-bearer would laugh feebly, to indicate it was all a little joke, and then rush off to find the solution himself. People thought Snodgrass was a genius and often wondered what great ideas he was mulling over as he puffed his pipe and looked thoughtful and bemused. Eventually, I would learn the truth: Doc Snodgrass was not smart enough to mull.

One example will serve to illustrate the effectiveness of the dean's approach to human relations.

During a campus uprising, the students demanded that the college administration do away with Poverty,

War, and Mashed Turnips in the Commissary, although not necessarily in that order. Doc Snodgrass appeared suddenly on the steps of the administration building, seemingly to confront the chanting mob but more likely because he had mistaken the exit for the door to the restroom. (His thoughtful expression was probably due at first to his wondering why so many students of both sexes were in the men's room.) As he fumbled about in his pockets looking for his tobacco pouch—the search for the source of the Nile took scarcely longer—the students fell silent, no doubt saving their breath for the purpose of shouting down the words of wisdom they expected to be forthcoming from the dean. (Youths are not called callow for nothing.) The pouch at last found, the dean began to fill his pipe, tamping and filling, tamping and filling, and all the while looking extremely thoughtful. Then he began probing his pockets for a match. Finally, an exasperated student in guerrilla attire lunged forward and thrust upon him a disposable lighter, little realizing that the dean was confounded by all such modern technology. His efforts to ignite the lighter by scratching it against a brick wall produced a good laugh from the students and a consensus among them that anyone with a sense of humor like that couldn't be such a bad guy after all. The mood of the crowd lightened. A game of Frisbee broke out. Someone threw a football. A coed burned her bra.

Having solved the riddle of the lighter, and tortured the tobacco into a state of combustion, Snodgrass began sucking away on his pipe as he looked increasingly thoughtful. He was, as I say, a master of the thoughtful expression. Even the hardliners among the students seemed unable to resist the impression that the dean was contemplating the eradication of Poverty, War, and Mashed Turnips. The crowd began to disperse, its members exchanging among themselves the opinion that the dean had not only a great sense of humor but a mind "like a steel trap." The truth was, he had a mind like flypaper, and not very good flypaper at that. His total intellectual arsenal consisted of his pipe and those two facial expressions.

The import of the dean's pipe did not strike me immediately, but when it did, I rushed out and bought myself a pipe and tobacco and began practicing my expressions. As a direct consequence of these efforts, I began rising through the professorial ranks as if by levitation. The ugly rumor that I had flunked three successive IQ tests (there were a lot of trick questions) was silenced once and for all. Faculty and students alike began referring to me as one who had a mind like a steel trap. And I continued to puff my pipe and look alternately bemused and thoughtful as promotion after promotion was thrust upon me. Still, not all was well. There was the problem of my ineptitude at outdoor sports.

Then one day I was struck by a marvelous idea. If my pipe and expressions had worked so well in advancing my career, why wouldn't they be equally effective in something worthwhile, such as hunting and fishing? The very next weekend, on a fishing trip with Retch Sweeney and Fenton Quagmire, I took along my pipe and tobacco and, of course, my ability to become bemused or thoughtful at the drop of a hat.

The fishing started out routinely, with Sweeney and Quagmire making snide remarks about my casting technique. For the most part, however, they confined their merriment to a few chortles, saving the belly laughs for the embarrassing predicament that my lack of coordination invariably lands me in.

Presently, I spotted a promising patch of water, but it was made almost inaccessible because of thick brush and high banks on one side and a monstrous logjam on the other. For that very reason I guessed that the deep hole beneath the logjam probably hadn't been prospected recently by other anglers. As I studied the situation, I noticed a slender log jutting out through the brush on the bank, and I quickly calculated that by sitting on the end of this log I could cast over the hole and still remain concealed from the fish. Five minutes later I was perched somewhat precariously on the end of the log and, in fact, had already extracted a couple of plump trout from beneath the logjam. Sweeney and Quagmire, both as yet without a single strike, glared enviously at me and cursed my ingenuity. Now it was my turn to chortle. But right in the middle of my chortle, a huge rainbow zoomed out of the depths like a Polaris missile and detonated on my Black Gnat. This was exactly what I had been anticipating, and with lightning reflexes, I fell off the log and dropped fifteen feet into a bed of assorted boulders, none smaller than a breadbox. Even though my impact on the rocks caused me to wonder momentarily whether pelvic transplants had yet been perfected, I immediately arose without so much as a whimper, whipped out my pipe, and began stuffing it with tobacco. Already I detected the sounds of Sweeney and Quagmire crashing through the brush, possibly to determine if I had suffered any serious injury but more likely racing each other for the fishing spot I had so recently abandoned. In any case, I knew that great booming laughs were already gestating in their bellies.

But I was ready. When their heads popped from the brush, I was calmly puffing on my pipe and looking thoughtfully up at the log.

"You hurt?" Sweeney asked, traces of a smile already playing in the corners of his mouth.

To such a question I normally would have snappishly replied, "No, you idiot, I've always been shaped like a potato chip!" Then would have come the wild howls of mirth, the ecstatic knee-slapping, and the attempts by Sweeney and Quagmire to re-create through mimicry some of my more extravagant moves during the course of the fall. But not this time.

Calmly, I blew a puff of smoke toward them and displayed my bemused look. I then returned my thoughtful gaze to the log.

I will not exaggerate the quality of my companions' mental processes by suggesting that they had flashes of insight. Nevertheless, I sensed some faint cognitive flickerings.

"Whatcha do that for?" asked Quagmire, referring to my fall.

"Yeah, you could've hurt yourself," Sweeney added, puzzled.

Without replying, I continued to study the log thoughtfully, occasionally tossing a bemused look in the direction of my audience of two.

Thoroughly befuddled, Quagmire and Sweeney at last wandered off to resume their fishing. They clearly were of the impression that I had deliberately planned and executed the fall from the log, possibly as a scientific experiment for a secret government agency. Success! Before shouting "Eureka!" however, I salved my injuries with emergency first aid, which consisted largely of defoliating all the flora within a five-foot radius by hissing a stream of colorful expressions, and hopping about like a rain dancer trying to terminate a five-year drought.

I could scarcely wait to test the pipe-and-two-expression ploy on wits quicker than those of Sweeney and Quagmire. The next weekend I was fishing alone on one of my favorite rivers and happened to run into a chap whose name turned out to be Shep. He obviously was an expert fly caster. His wrist would twitch and eighty feet of line would shoot toward the far bank, the tiny fly settling on the surface of the water as softly as a falling flake of dandruff. Even as I watched, he netted one of the finest trout I've ever seen taken from the river.

"I think I'll keep this one," he said to me. "Now the big ones, I always release them."

"Big ones?" I said, ogling his hefty catch. "Why, yes, I never take any of the big ones home myself. In fact, I often don't take home any small ones or middle-sized ones either."

"Now, that's what I call true sportsmanship!" Shep said, casually dropping a fly three inches from the far bank. "Say, there's plenty of room here. Why don't you try a few casts yourself?"

I had already dug out my pipe and lighted up. "Well, maybe, but first let me see you do that again, that, uh, cast of yours."

He obliged me with a repeat performance, this time placing the fly a mere inch from the bank. I puffed my pipe and gave him my bemused look.

"Something wrong?" he asked, a note of unease in his voice.

I puffed away, looking bemused, as he made another awesome cast. He was showing definite signs of discomfort.

"It's my elbow, isn't it?" he said. "I've never held my elbow the way you're supposed to. Maybe you can give me a couple of lessons."

I knocked the ashes out of my pipe, changed to the thoughtful expression, and unleashed a powerful twenty-foot cast, the splash from which lifted a flock of crows cawing into the air from a nearby cornfield.

Shep leaped back. "Are you okay? That was a nasty spasm you had just then."

I silenced him with my bemused look. Then I stoked up my pipe again, alternating between thoughtful and bemused expressions. That destroyed the last of Shep's confidence. Ten minutes later I had him totally under my power and was even giving him a few casting tips.

"There you go again," I scolded him, "casting over twenty-five feet. You have to learn control, man, learn control!"

"I know," Shep said, whimpering, "but I just can't seem to get the knack of it."

"Well, then, try this approach," I advised. "Just pretend you're a little old lady fighting off a bee with a broom handle."

Naturally, I was delighted to discover that this bit of business with the pipe and two expressions not only transcended my lack of coordination but conveyed the impression that I was actually an expert angler. Within six months, I had applied the technique to all the other outdoor sports and found that it worked equally well. Now when I missed an easy shot at a pheasant, say, I would no longer hang my head and look embarrassed. Instead, I'd stick the pipe in my mouth and look bemused. "You sure scared the heck out of that ol' ring-neck," my companion would say. "You've got to be darn good to miss a shot like that!"

To date, my greatest achievement with the pipe and two expressions occurred on a backpacking trip into a wilderness area of the Rocky Mountains. Sweeney, Quagmire, and I were hiking along a trail when we came across a bear track of approximately the dimensions of a doormat.

"Bleep!" hissed Sweeney. "Look at the size of that track!"

"It's fr-fresh, too," whispered Quagmire, swiveling his head about. "L-looks like grizzly. Can't be far away, either."

As I now do under all such circumstances, I dug out the pipe, calmly filled, tamped, and lighted it. Just then a grouse exploded from the brush at the edge of the trail and gave all three of us quite a start. Nevertheless, I puffed away on my pipe and looked bemused. Both Quagmire and Sweeney said later they were extremely impressed by my reaction. After all, it's no simple thing to puff a pipe and look bemused when you're running that fast.

Poof—No Eyebrows!

Just as I was assembling the ingredients for a small snack in the kitchen, the doorbell rang. My wife, Bun, went to answer it, and I heard her invite in Milt Slapshot, a neighbor who often seeks out my advice on matters pertaining to the sporting life.

"Is Pat home?" I heard Milt ask. "A fella told me he knows something about muzzleloading."

Realizing Bun could never resist a straight line like that, I jumped up and headed for the living room in the hope of stifling her.

"Does he ever!" she said, chortling. "Why, this very minute he's out in the kitchen loading his muzzle!"

A wife who chortles is an irritation, but one who also regards herself as a wit is a social nuisance. I grabbed Milt by the arm and guided him toward the den before Bun could embarrass the poor fellow further with another attempt at emulating Erma Bombeck.

"Stop the cackling, Milt," I told him. "It only encourages her."

Once his tasteless display of mirth had subsided, Milt explained that he was building a muzzleloader and needed some technical advice from me. A mutual acquaintance, one Retch Sweeney, had told him that I had once conducted extensive scientific research on primitive firearms. That was true. In fact, it would be difficult to find firearms more primitive than those utilized in my research.

"You've come to the right man," I said. "Yes, indeed. Now the first thing I need to know is, are you building it from a kit or from scratch?"

"A kit," Milt said.

"Good," I said. "Building muzzleloaders from scratch is a risky business, particularly when you work your way up to sewer pipe too soon. Now the first thing . . ."

"Sewer pipe?" Milt asked. "What do you mean, sewer pipe? Are you sure you know something about black powder?"

"Ha!" I replied. "Do you see my eyebrows?"

"No."

"Well, that should answer your question. All us experts on black powder have bald eyes."

Actually, I do have eyebrows, but they are pale, sickly fellows, never having recovered from the shock of instant immolation thirty years ago. Having my eyebrows catch fire ranks as one of the more interesting experiences of my life, although I must say I didn't enjoy it much at the time.

Indeed, my somewhat faulty eyesight may be a direct result of having my eyebrows go up in smoke. Either it was that or the splash of Orange Crush soda pop with which my sidekick Retch Sweeney, ever quick to compound a catastrophe, doused the flames.

As I explained to Milt, who had settled into a chair in the den and was attempting with some success to conceal his fascination, most of my early research into the mysteries of black powder took place during the year I was fourteen. Some of those experiments produced spectacular results, particularly the last one, which enabled Retch and me to attend the annual Halloween party as twin cinders.

The first experiment, in which my eyebrows were sacrificed to the cause of science, consisted of placing a small pile of black powder on a bicycle seat and touching a lighted match to it. I can no longer recall why a bicycle seat was employed as part of the apparatus, but I am sure my co-researcher and I had sound reasons for it at the time. In any case, we proved conclusively that a match flame serves as an excellent catalyst on gunpowder. I later concluded that the experiment might have been improved upon in only two ways: to have placed the powder on *Retch's* bicycle seat and to have let *him* hold the match. Instead, he chose to stand in awe of the experiment and about ten feet away, sucking absently on a bottle of Orange Crush. On the other hand, my sacrifice was not without its reward, since bald eyes and a hole burnt in my bicycle seat made great conversation openers with girls at school.

The success of the experiment had to be withheld from the rest of the scientific community for fear our parents would find out about it. Unfortunately, my mother inadvertently discovered the secret.

"Is anything the matter?" Mom asked during supper the evening after the bicycle-seat experiment.

"No," I replied casually. "Why do you ask?"

"Oh, nothing in particular," she said. "It just seems a little odd, your wearing sunglasses and a cap at the dinner table."

She then expressed her desire that I remove both glasses and cap instantly, sooner if possible. After some debate over the finer points of dinner-table propriety, I complied.

As expected, Mom responded with the classic question favored by the parents of young black powder experimenters everywhere: "WHAT HAPPENED TO YOUR EYEBROWS?"

Looking surprised and fingering the scorched area above my eyes, I tried to convey the impression that it was news to me that my eyebrows were missing, as if they might have dropped off unnoticed or been mislaid at school.

The truth was soon extracted from me with an efficiency that would have been the envy of medieval counterintelligence agents. This was followed by a bit of parental advice. But scarcely had this parental advice ceased reverberating among the rafters than I was already plotting my next experiments for unlocking the mysteries of black powder.

The discovery by Retch and me that we could purchase black powder in bulk from a local dealer was to have great impact on our lives, not to mention various parts of our anatomies. The dealer in question was the proprietor of Grogan's War Surplus, Hardware & Gun Emporium, none other than that old reprobate, Henry P. Grogan himself. We weren't at all sure Grogan would sell a couple of scruffy, goof-off kids something as potentially dangerous as black powder. Our first attempt at making a purchase was, therefore, cloaked in subtlety and subterfuge.

"Howdy, Mr. Grogan," we opened with, both of us so casual we were fit to burst.

"Howdy, boys. What can I do for you—assuming, of course, you got cash in your pockets and ain't just here to finger the merchandise?"

"Oh, we got cash," I said. "Uh, Retch, why don't you read Mr. Grogan our list?"

"Uh, okay, heh, heh. Yeah, well, here goes—one GI mess kit, one helmet liner, a parachute harness, a pound of black powder, and let's see, now, do you have any of those neat camouflage jackets left?"

To our chagrin, a look of concern came into Grogan's eyes. "Gosh, boys, I don't know if I should . . . It just don't seem right to sell you two young fellows . . . Oh, what the heck! Elmer Peabody wanted me to save those last two camouflage jackets for him, but I'll let you have 'em. Now, how much gunpowder was that you wanted—a pound?"

In all fairness to Grogan, I must admit that he did warn us that severe bodily harm could result from improper use of the black powder. His exact words, if I remember correctly, were, "You boys set off any of that stuff near my store and I'll peel your hides!"

The black powder we bought from Grogan had been compressed by the manufacturer into shiny black pellets, a form intended, I believe, to make it less volatile. Even before mashing them into powder, we found it was possible to touch off the pellets if they were first piled on a bicycle seat and a match held to them. The pellets did not ignite immediately even then, apparently for the purpose of tricking the person holding the match into taking a closer look at what was occurring on the bicycle seat. Then—*poof!*—no eyebrows.

Our first muzzleloaders were small and crude, but as our technological skill and knowledge increased, they gradually became large and crude. We never did develop a satisfactory triggering mechanism. On the average shot, you could eat a sandwich between the time the trigger was pulled and the gun discharged. A typical muzzleloader test would go something like this:

RETCH: Okay, I'm going to squeeze the trigger now. There!

MUZZLELOADER: *Snick! Pop! Ssssss . . .*

ME: Good. It looks like it's working. Better start aiming at the tin can.

MUZZLELOADER: *Ssss . . . fizt . . . ssss . . .*

RETCH: Say, give me a bit of that sandwich, will you?

ME: Sure.

MUZZLELOADER: *. . . sss . . . sput . . . ss . . . putt . . . ss . . .*

RETCH: What time is it?

ME: About time for me to—

MUZZLELOADER: *. . . ssst—POOT!*

RETCH (enveloped in cloud of smoke): How was my aim?

ME: I think it was pretty good, but the muzzle velocity leaves something to be desired. As soon as the smoke clears, reach over and pick up the ball and we'll load her up again.

Even as we increased the range of our muzzleloaders, the delay in the firing mechanism discouraged us from using them on game. If we had used one of them for rabbit hunting, say, we would have had to squeeze the trigger and then hope a rabbit would happen to be running by when the gun discharged. Squeezing the trigger before your game appears over the far horizon is the ultimate in leading a moving target.

Since we had up to three minutes of lead time on stationary targets, hunting with our muzzleloaders seemed somewhat impractical. There was also the probable embarrassment of having our shots bounce off the game. It didn't seem worth the risk. A hunter can stand only so much humiliation.

Our first muzzleloader was a small-caliber derringer, the ammunition for which consisted mostly of dried peas. This prompted Retch to remark derisively to a tin-can target, "All right, Ringo, drop your iron or I'll fill you full of dried peas."

"Okay, okay," I said, "I get your drift. We'll move up to the hard stuff—marbles, ball bearings, golf balls."

It was a mistake, though, and I knew it. Once you start escalating, there's no stopping until you achieve the ultimate weapon. Within a couple of months, we were turning out muzzleloaders in the .80-caliber range. Then we got into the large-caliber stuff. Finally, we decided the time had come to stop monkeying around with black powder pistols and rifles. We'd had some close calls. We had reached the point where there was some doubt in our minds whether we might be firing a muzzleloader or touching off a bomb. Thus it was with considerable relief that we abandoned our clandestine manufacture and testing of pistols and rifles. After all, a cannon would be much safer; you didn't have to hold it.

The cannon was constructed of sewer pipe, two-by-fours, baby-carriage wheels, rubber inner-tube bands, a clothespin, baling wire, and various other odds and ends, all of which, blending into a single, symmetrical unity, neared perfection on the scale of beauty. A croquet ball was commandeered from the Sweeney backyard for use as shot. In our enthusiasm of the moment, it was thought the croquet ball could be returned to the set after it was recovered from the firing range. Alas, it was not to be so.

Attired in our muskrat-skin hats, which we had sewn up ourselves, we mounted our bicycles and, with cannon in tow, set off for the local golf course, where a fairway would serve as a firing range, a putting green as a target.

As we had hoped, the golf course turned out to be deserted. We quickly wheeled the cannon into firing position and began the loading procedure.

"Think that's enough powder?" Retch asked.

"Better dump in some more," I advised. "That croquet ball is pretty heavy."

"And there's some for good measure," Retch said.

The croquet ball fit a little too tightly, but we managed to ram it down the barrel.

Then we both took up positions alongside the cannon to witness the rare and wonderful spectacle of a sewer pipe firing a croquet ball down a golf-course fairway.

"Ready, aim, fire!" I commanded.

Retch tripped the firing mechanism.

Eventually, the thunder was replaced by clanging bells inside our heads, the shattered pieces of earth and sky fell back into place, and the wobbly world righted itself. Retch and I limped over to the side of a utility shed and sat down to relax a bit and collect our senses. Presently, a deputy sheriff drove up. He stood for a moment gazing at the haze of smoke wafting gently over the golf course, the patch of smoldering turf ringed by fragments of sewer pipe, baby-carriage wheels, and pieces of two-by-four. Then, hoisting up his gun belt, he sauntered over to us.

"You boys know anything about an explosion out this way?" he asked.

"What kind of explosion?" Retch asked.

"A *big* explosion."

I was still so stunned I couldn't even think up a good lie. Anyway, I knew the deputy had us cold.

"Now, what I want to know," the deputy went on, "is why are you two boys sitting out here behind this shed smoking?"

"Shucks," I said, "if you'd been a little earlier, you'd have seen us while we were still on fire!"

I thought for sure he was going to haul us off to jail, but instead he just smiled, took one last look at the smoldering debris, and started to saunter back to his car. "Well, if you fellas turn up any information about the explosion," he said over his shoulder, "I'd appreciate it if you'd let me know. I don't reckon there'll be another one, do you?"

"Nope," Retch and I said in unison.

Then the deputy stopped and kicked gingerly at something on the ground in front of him. It was Retch's muskrat hat! The deputy turned and gave us a sympathetic look. "Too bad about your dog," he said.

The cannon pretty well quelled our enthusiasm for building our own muzzleloaders from scratch. Not only had it made a big impression on us; it had made numerous small impressions. Years later, while I was undergoing a physical examination, the doctor commented on some bumps under my skin.

"Pay them no mind, doc," I told him. "They're just pieces of sewer pipe."

At this juncture of my recitation, Milt Slapshot jumped up and headed for the door.

"Thanks," he said. "You've answered my question."

"Gee," I said. "I've even forgotten what the question was. But if you need any help putting your muzzleloader kit together, Milt, just give me a call."

He hasn't called yet. I suppose he's been tied up at the office a lot lately.

I Fish;
Therefore, I Am

Scholars have long known that fishing eventually turns men into philosophers. Unfortunately, it is almost impossible to buy decent tackle on a philosopher's salary. I have always thought it would be better if fishing turned men into Wall Street bankers, but that is not the case. It's philosophers or nothing.

I became a philosopher at age twelve, after a scant six years of fishing. One evening at supper I looked up from my plate and announced, "I fish; therefore, I am." Perhaps awed by this evidence of precocity in a young boy, my stepfather turned to my mother and asked, "Is there any more gravy?" Thus encouraged, I forgot about philosophy until I went off to college.

The intellectual experience of life in a college dorm proved to be enormously stimulating, and soon I was engaged in a variety of scientific experiments. My research paper, "Levitation: A Roommate's Response to a Garter Snake in His Bed," caught the fancy of a psychology professor who invited me to join him in research on abnormal behavior in lesser primates. Three months later, I made a remarkable discovery. If I pressed either the red or green buttons, nothing happened, but if I pressed the yellow, a bunch of bananas would drop out of a hole in the ceiling. Not caring much for bananas, I resigned my position and went in search of more serious, if not more fruitful, studies.

While trying to decide on a major in college, I picked up a minor in philosophy, one Maylene Whipple by name, who could have passed for twenty-five any day of the week. It came as a shock to me to learn that the precocious Maylene was only seventeen, particularly since we had already engaged in discourse on the Hegelian dialectic, which is a felony in most states even if committed by consenting adults. Maylene was amazed at my grasp of all the world's great philosophies, but less so at my grasp of her left knee, to which she responded with a karate chop that left my wrist bones in shambles.

"Where did you learn so much about philosophy?" Maylene asked, as I smiled suavely, clutching my throbbing wrist in an armpit.

"From fishing," I said. "I started fishing at age six, and by the time I was twelve, I was a full-fledged philosopher."

"Pooh!" she said. "Fishing can't turn you into a philosopher!"

"Oh yeah!" I said. "How about Francis Bacon? How about him?"

"What about Francis Bacon?"

"Why, Bacon was nothing but a humble tailor until he took up fishing. Five years later, he invented the scientific method and changed the course of history, despite never having landed a brown trout over fourteen inches."

"That's incredible!" Maylene gasped.

"Yes," I replied, "particularly when you consider there were plenty of really big brown trout around back then. The rule is, however, The worse the fisherman, the better the philosopher."

I went on to explain to Maylene that Aristotle was known among his associates merely as "one weird dude" until he met up with Plato. "Teach me to be a philosopher," Aristotle pleaded.

Plato was immediately intrigued by the young man. "All right," he said. "Let us begin with the basics: Truth, Justice, and How to Bait a Hook Properly."

Plato himself was so miserably inept at fishing that he eventually wrote *The Republic,* which is just about as bad as you can get when it comes to catching fish. Much to Plato's disappointment, *The Republic* was rejected by all the leading outdoor publications of the day.

"That sounds pretty fishy to me," Maylene said.

"Yes," I replied. "That is what I am trying to tell you. All philosophy is pretty fishy underneath."

"Underneath what?" Maylene asked.

"I don't know that yet," I said. "I'm only a sophomore."

And I was to remain a sophomore for several years, largely as a result of my study of philosophy at every lake and stream within a hundred miles of the university. The one great universal question I sought to answer was why the angler always should have been here last week.

After graduation, I studied with the great French existential philosopher Albert Camus, who told me that men must learn to live without hope.

"Why is that?" I asked, disentangling a backlash.

Taking advantage of the opportunity afforded by my backlash, Camus cast into the hole in which I had just had a nice strike. "Because that way, even if you don't catch any fish, you're never disappointed. You can always say you just enjoyed being out communing with nature on a nice day. Catching fish is not a matter of ultimate concern, unless, of course, we are talking about something over five pounds."

The other great French existential philosopher, Jean-Paul Sartre, once gave me an analogy to explain his concepts of Being and Nothingness. "This," he said, holding up a stick with one paltry eight-inch trout on it, "is Being. That," he said, pointing to my empty creel, "is Nothingness."

I have studied the philosophy of Karl Marx at considerable length, and although I understand it has gained a number of followers in certain parts of the world, I personally have never found it appealing, perhaps because I disagree with one of its basic tenets. Marx believed that anglers should put all their bait in the same can, from which each would take according to his need. I, on the other hand, believe that each fisherman should dig and fish his own worms, although I am not averse to going sharesies on the fly book of a really good tyer.

William James's philosophy of pragmatism was more to my liking. Pragmatism is the philosophy of doing that which works, no matter what your mother might have told you. James, who had pretensions of being a dry-fly purist, developed pragmatism from a simple experiment he performed one fishless day on a trout stream. He discovered that by making a slight modification in a No. 18 Caddis, he was suddenly catching monstrous brook trout. The James Ploy, as the experiment came to be called, is still popular with some fishermen, even though the technical difficulty of attaching a night crawler to a No. 18 Caddis has never been solved.

Ludwig Wittgenstein once explained logical positivism to me in a way that made it seem the answer to all the great philosophical questions, except what to do about spilled tackle boxes.

Morris Lippenstein, a friend of mine in college, developed the philosophy of transactional redundance. It was a lousy philosophy, but Morris, on the other hand, was a terrific fisherman. Even now his former professors still refer to him as "Morris the Sophomore."

The best philosopher I've ever known was a man by the name of Rancid Crabtree. Rancid lived in a little cabin in the woods behind our place when I was a boy, and since his time was free of all forms of gainful employment, he was able to devote himself to philosophy for up to twelve hours a day, not including cleaning and eating the catch. As a student of philosophy, I often sat at the feet of this great teacher, although I preferred a chair situated some distance upwind.

Rancid was at his philosophical best while on a trout stream.

"The water's a little murky for good fishing," I observed once.

Rancid took a chaw of tobacco and studied the water. "Ain't nothin' never just right to do what you wants to do when you wants to do it," he philosophized. "So you best just go ahead and do it anyways."

"Spinoza?" I asked.

"Naw, just a little tobaccy juice dribblin' down my chin."

Although Rancid's philosophy seemed to be centered on fishing, it shaped much of my attitude toward life. Here is a sampling of his philosophy:

"The two best times to fish is when it's rainin' and when it ain't."

"Smoked carp tastes just as good as smoked salmon when you ain't got no smoked salmon."

"There ain't no private property you cain't fish if you knows how to hunker a spell with the man what owns it."

"You cain't make fish bite just by wantin' 'em to."

"Any time a man ain't fishin' he's fritterin' away his life."

As I say, Rancid Crabtree's philosophy had an enormous influence on me. If it hadn't been for that, I might now be living a life adorned with the tawdry baubles of wealth, a life made sleazy and decadent by conspicuous consumption. I might even have turned out to be one of the jaded beautiful people of the jet set. Other than those drawbacks, Rancid's philosophy has served me pretty well.

Running on Empty

Some of the boys and I were sitting around Kelly's Bar & Grill the other evening, stretching and varnishing a few truths about our adventures in the Great Outdoors, when Kelly himself hauled a new round of iced schooners over to our table and sat down. He listened to the conversation for a few moments, shaking his head in a pretty good impression of annoyance and then muttered, "Fish, hunt, fish, hunt! Can't you guys ever talk about anything else?"

"You don't care much for outdoor sports, do you, Kelly?" Retch Sweeney asked.

"Oh, you guys are all right," Kelly said. "It's just that I can't understand what you see in hunting and fishing. Man, that stuff is boring!"

"Maybe to you it's boring," Al Finley put in, "but to us it's exciting."

"Ha!" Kelly said. "Exciting! Listen, I know, I fished once. It's boring!"

"Is not!" Al said.

"*Is!*" said Kelly. "Okay, wise guys, tell me, what's the most exciting thing about hunting and fishing?"

I thought for a moment. "Running out of gas."

The other guys all nodded in agreement.

"Running out of gas?" asked Kelly, astonished. "I would've thought something like being chased by a big bear."

"That's a good one, too," I said. "But for absolute, undiluted, marrow-chilling excitement, it's running out of gas."

"I can't believe I'm sitting here listening to this nonsense," Kelly snarled. With that, he got up and stomped back to the bar to spit-polish some glasses.

Like Kelly, most people unfamiliar with outdoor sports find it hard to believe that running out of gas is the most exciting part of hunting and fishing. That's because they know only about the typical, mundane experience of running out of gas on a well-traveled highway, such as happened to me just the other day.

On my way home from a business trip, I thought I could make it across a desert without being ripped off for a tankful at one of those seedy "Last Chance for Gas" places that loiter on the edge of deserts. A mere fifteen miles from the next gas station, my car choked, coughed a few times, and then chugged to a stop. Heat waves rippled up from the empty horizon and gusts of searing wind sandblasted my car. It was all I could do to keep from laughing. "You call this running out of gas?" I said to the fates that govern such things. "This is child's play!"

I then nonchalantly flagged down the eighty-seventh car to pass, a vehicle driven, as I judged, by a recent escapee from an institution for the criminally insane.

The man's conversation was diverting, based as it was on a considerable expertise in the use of poisons, stilettos, hatchets, and pipe bombs. Some twenty months later, we arrived at the gas station, where he dropped me off. When I thanked him for the ride and for sparing my life, he snapped his fingers as though reminded of some forgotten business, then drove off in a huff, apparently much disgusted with himself.

The gas station attendant, on the other hand, proved difficult. He said his station had a policy against providing any aid whatsoever to travelers in perilous distress, including the loaning out of tools, the restroom key, or containers in which to carry gas back to stranded vehicles. Without much coaxing, however, he agreed to sell me a rusty little gas can, a family heirloom, as he said, which his great-grandfather had had handcrafted of rare metals by a team of silversmiths imported from Switzerland. Snatching up my heirloom of gas, I hoofed it back to my car in a trice or, to be more specific, four hours and ten minutes. Although the trek was long and hot, the buzzards circling overhead afforded some shade, and I could not help but think how accustomed we are to zipping mindlessly along in our shiny tin capsules, totally oblivious to the ever-changing face of nature; and what a good thing it is, too.

For an outdoorsman, though, that sort of running out of gas doesn't even rank as a nuisance, let alone excitement. It requires no skill, no finesse. It is an accident, a result of faulty judgment, a miscalculation. The outdoorsman cannot leave such an important part of his avocation to mere chance. He must plan and practice his routine until he gets it perfect. Then, finally, when he has mastered the art, he can drive his vehicle to the far end of a wilderness canyon and, some fifty miles or so beyond the boundaries of the known world, with night closing in and storm clouds rising, turn to his companions and, with just the right degree of flair, announce, "G-great jumping gosh almighty, I think we're out of g-gas!"

Nothing so stirs the emotions and invigorates the vitals of an outdoorsman as that announcement, particularly when it is enhanced by a sappy, bug-eyed expression on the face of the announcer. Once the announcement has been made, the tradition is that the other persons in the car are supposed to respond in unison, "Ooooh *bleep!*" Sometimes, though, they merely sit there slack-jawed, staring at the gas gauge in disbelief. Also, on occasion, they will choose to unwind with a bit of horseplay, such as taking turns chasing the vehicle's driver and trying to hit him with a stick.

There are numerous ways of running out of gas in the wilderness. One of the best is to run over large, sharp rocks that puncture your gas tank. This method usually affords a much greater degree of surprise, since all the gas dribbles quietly out onto the ground while you are away from the car getting cold, hungry, and exhausted in the pursuit of fish or game. It is considered poor form, however, to clap your hands and emit happy yelps of surprise over the discovery that you ruptured the gas tank on some sharp rocks. The time is better employed getting a head start down the road while your companions are still selecting their sticks and testing them for tensile strength.

The problem with the punctured-gas-tank method is that you can't always depend on finding large, sharp rocks in the right places. Thus, running out of gas a sufficient distance out in the boonies to qualify you as a master of the art becomes largely a matter of chance. The punctured tank is fine, if the opportunity offers itself, but should not be counted upon.

The so-called short cut, on the other hand, is practically foolproof, and I highly recommend it. The "short cut" is usually recalled by one of the members of the party as a road he was told about in a bar by a fellow who discovered it while huckleberrying with his family at age six. The "short cut" sounds like a reasonable option to the driver, particularly if he hasn't filled his quota for running out of gas that year. "It will cut our driving time in half," he explains, and of course, it does. The rest of the time is spent walking, usually up an incline that appears to be leading to the Continental Divide.

Another good method involves the use of an auxiliary gas tank. When the vehicle stalls, the driver says to his nervous company, "Oh-oh, Fred, looks like we're out of gas." Allowing himself the enjoyment of seeing perspiration bead up nicely on the passenger's forehead, the driver then chuckles and says, "Only joshing, Fred. Now, I'll just switch over to the auxiliary tank." The trick here, of course, is to have neglected to check the auxiliary tank after your kid borrowed your vehicle to go out for a pizza and failed to mention that the pizza was on the other side of the state. Because your partner may not see the humor in the situation, you should be prepared to entertain him with some of your impersonations of famous personalities.

The next best thing to running out of gas is *almost* running out of gas. Fraught with suspense, these trips are often referred to as *white-knucklers*. The term is derived from the driver's tendency to increase the tightness of his grip on the steering wheel in direct ratio to the rate the gas is diminishing. One theory holds that as much as fifteen additional miles can be squeezed out of the steering wheel itself. Further mileage is gained by all the passengers rocking forward in unison and chanting "C'mon, baby, c'mon!" Chanting by itself is not good for more than two additional miles.

Because it may be difficult for the non-outdoorsman to understand the exhilaration we hunters and anglers get from running out of gas, I will give an example from my own personal experience. Al Finley, Retch Sweeney, and I had just returned to my car from a fishing trip into the Hoodoo Mountains and were heading back to the main highway when I noticed the needle on the gas gauge was hovering half an inch below the empty mark. Immediately, I took the recommended emergency measure, which consists of beating on the gas gauge with your fist in an effort to get the needle to rise up to the point where you have enough gas to get home. I then fell back on squeezing the steering wheel, while Retch and Al rocked and chanted. But it was all to no avail. The engine inhaled the last vapors from the carburetor and died.

We sat there for a few moments, coining some colorful phrases, and then Al asked the usual question: "Well, what are we going to do now?"

"Beats me," I said.

"I got an idea," Retch said. "How far back was that big old house we passed?"

"About five miles, I'd guess," said Al.

"You mean that big spooky old house with the porch caving in and the shingles falling off?" I asked, hoping to diffuse the hostility in the car with some casual conversation. "Boy, I wonder what kind of person lives in a place like that. Pretty darn weird, I'll bet. And those dogs! Did you see those two big wolfy dogs, standing under that sign that said 'Trespassers will be shot'? I wonder what they were gnawing on. Looked like it was wearing a hat! Hoo-boy, I would no more go into that place than—what? What do you mean, my fault? No. They probably wouldn't have any gas anyway and . . ."

A few hours later, I was back at the car with a can of gas. One of my pants legs was missing and the back had been ripped out of my shirt. Fortunately, I had finally been able to lose the dogs by circling through a swamp and wading up a creek before scaling the cliff. The sense of exhilaration was marvelous. For the first time since running out of gas on Bald Mountain, I felt fully and truly alive, except for the lower half of my body, which seemed pretty well shot.

"Any trouble?" Al asked.

"None to speak of," I said. "Just the usual."

"Fella lives in that house," said Retch, "pretty weird, was he?"

"Just the usual. He wouldn't take any pay for the gas, though."

"No kidding!"

"Yeah, but be careful of that gas can. It's a family heirloom."

The Cat and the Cat Burglar

The sound of a vase crashing to the floor in the living room snapped my wife and me bolt upright in bed.

"It's the cat," Bun hissed. "You forgot to put the cat out again!"

"Oh, go back to sleep," I said. "It's probably only another burglar."

"You're trying to make excuses. I know it's the cat. You forgot to put it out!"

"Well, I'll prove it's a burglar," I growled, crawling out of bed and switching on the hall light. As I expected, a dark figure was wandering about the living room. "Hey you!"

The burglar pointed a questioning finger at his chest.

"Yes, you," I snapped. "You see anybody else in the living room? Now c'mere. I want to prove to my wife you're only a burglar and not the dang cat. Besides, there's no point in eyeing the TV—it blew a tube on California during the Miss America Pageant, which made two of us, heh, heh."

The burglar shuffled down the hall, a can of Blackjack Mugger's Spray trained on me. "Don't try no funny stuff."

"It was only a little joke."

"I know, but it was pretty bad, and I'm not up to it. I've had a hard night. How come your house is so empty?"

"We've had a lot of other burglaries," I explained. "For a while they were so frequent we thought about asking the burglars to each take a number so there wouldn't be so many here at one time."

"What did I say about da funny stuff?"

"Sorry. Say, I'd appreciate it if you would poke your head in the bedroom there so my wife will know you're only a burglar and not the cat."

The burglar peered cautiously around the door and looked at my wife.

"Oh, thank goodness you really are only a burglar," Bun said. "That cat makes such a terrible mess when it gets left in. My nice rug in the living room—"

"Can it, lady!" the burglar ordered. "I ain't got time to hear about no cat messes."

"Have it your way," Bun said. "But I really should tell you about Felix. He sometimes—"

"I said, *can it!*"

"Well, if you're going to be rude, I'll just go back to sleep. The last few burglars we had were at least civil!"

"Sheesh, do I ever pick 'em," the burglar moaned. Then he turned to me. "Say, you're da outdoor writer, ain't ya?"

"Well, sort of," I replied.

"Yeah, dat's what I was told. All you outdoor writers got big gun collections. Let's have a look at yours."

My gun collection! For years I had worried that some burglar would discover my secret gun room and clean it out. Now, under the threat of bodily harm, I was being forced to reveal my hoard of priceless firearms.

"Oh, all right, follow me," I told the burglar.

I led the way to the den, pressed a hidden button, and a wall panel slid silently back, revealing the secret gun room. The burglar whistled his approval at this bit of architectural ingenuity.

"And there's my fabulous collection," I said, pointing to the gun cabinet.

"Dat's it?" the burglar gasped, awestruck.

"Yes," I said, "that's it. A fence will pay you handsomely for these fine guns. Your fortune is made, I'm afraid."

Unlocking the doors to the gun cabinet, I decided to take one last desperate chance to save my collection. "Why don't you sit down and make yourself comfortable," I said to the burglar, "and I'll tell you about these guns. Should you decide to keep them for your own enjoyment, knowing their histories will increase the pleasure of owning them."

Apparently approving of this suggestion, the burglar flopped into an armchair, while I removed one of my favorite rifles from the gun cabinet.

"If you were a connoisseur of fine guns," I began, "I would first tie a bib around your neck so you wouldn't drool all over your clothes when I showed you this little .30/30. Notice, if you will, the grip of the stock."

"Yeah, what caused dat, termites? Or did your dog chew it?"

"To the contrary," I replied, "this is custom checking on the grip, which in all modesty I must admit I accomplished myself with a ball-peen hammer and a five-penny nail. True, the exquisiteness of the pattern is detracted from somewhat by the wrappings of baling wire and electrician's tape on the stock. You may also have noticed that the barrel is slightly bent to the left and downward, but I can assure you it's not more than an inch out of alignment. I won't go into how the stock got splintered and the barrel bent except to say that it saved me from a nasty fall. The gun is still remarkably accurate, however, provided you make the necessary adjustments in your aim. I assume you have studied calculus? No? Well, perhaps one of those pocket calculators would work just as well, although a bit bothersome on a running shot."

Feigning disgust, the burglar motioned for me to return the .30/30 to the rack. He pointed to another rifle. "What's dat, a .30/06?"

"Close," I said. "Actually, it's a .30/02, one of the predecessors of the .30/06. There was a little problem with the locking mechanism on the bolt, and the model was discontinued when it was discovered that the breech velocity sometimes exceeded the muzzle velocity. Otherwise, it's perfectly safe, as long as you don't forget to jerk your head away the instant you squeeze the trigger. My grandfather once killed a trophy elk with the bolt when the animal tried to slip past him forty yards to the rear. But that kind of shooting takes considerable practice and I don't recommend it for beginners."

A hint of gloom had settled upon the burglar's

features as he gestured irritably for me to return the .30/02 to the cabinet.

I next took down a wonderful old side-by-side 12-gauge shotgun I also had inherited from my grandfather—"Old One-Ear" they called him—on my fourteenth birthday. As I told the burglar, the shotgun had one interesting little eccentricity, which was that on about every third shot both barrels discharged simultaneously regardless of which trigger was squeezed. Since I weighed only 125 pounds at the time, most student pilots log less flight time than I did on an average hunt, and their landings are a good deal softer.

As for the effects of these double-barreled kicks on my anatomy, the high school football coach once observed me coming out of the showers and leaped to the conclusion that I had contracted a progressive disease in which one shoulder takes on the general shape and color of a Hubbard squash. There was also the problem that my nose from week to week seemed to drift about my face, sometimes anchoring under my left eye and at other times setting a course for the center of my forehead. This feature was nicely complemented by my right ear, which appeared to have been run through a pasta-shaping machine.

"I used this fine old gun for nearly twenty years," I told the burglar. "But people were always asking me about the 'accident,' and I got tired of telling them I had saved my commanding officer in Korea by throwing myself on a hand grenade."

The burglar stifled a yawn with his fist. "C'mon, guy, I ain't got all night, ya know. Let's speed it up on dese histories, huh?"

"Right," I said. "I think you'll like this next one."

I unracked the single-shot .22 rifle that had been given to me by my parents when I was eleven years old. Ah, never was a gun given more tender care than that one. I cleaned and oiled it three times a day whether it had been fired or not, and never allowed a speck of dust to settle on it for more than a minute.

"So how come it's all rusted and pitted?" the burglar asked, his voice fairly reeking with exasperation, perhaps because I was delaying my account of the .22 in an unsuccessful attempt to wrench the bolt back.

As I told the burglar, a couple of months after the .22 had come into my possession, I was out in the back pasture target-practicing on a tin can when who should show up but a neighbor by the name of Olga Bonemarrow. I didn't much care for girls at the time, and considered Olga in particular a great nuisance. Ignoring her, I continued to plink away at the can while she directed a torrent of prattle at the back of my head. Suddenly a single question leaped from the torrent like a sparkling cutthroat from the spring runoff.

"Do you want to come over to my house and play doctor?" Olga had asked.

By sheer coincidence, Olga had hit upon one of my great enthusiasms of the moment, namely the field of medicine. Such was my passion for the art and science of curing the sick that target practice and even my beloved .22 were immediately blotted from my consciousness. Attempting to comport myself in a dignified manner appropriate to a serious student of medicine, I raced panting after Olga to her house, where we slipped upstairs to her bedroom without detection by Mr. and Mrs. Bonemarrow.

While I grabbed a window curtain and dried my palms, which were sweating profusely from the previous exertion, Olga rummaged around under her bed, finally extracting a large flat box. The box for a moment consumed one hundred percent of my attention, for on its lid was printed the word "Doctor." Olga took off the lid, removed a board zigzagged with lines of squares, placed two tiny white wooden figures on the square bearing the title "Med School," and then began to shuffle little stacks of cards. Even as I sized up the situation, my interest in the field of medicine began to fall off sharply.

"I just remembered a previous engagement," I told Olga and headed for the door.

"Hold it, buster," Olga snapped, adding with ominous vagueness, "or I'll tell Pa!"

Pa, I should point out, was built like a nail keg and had a temper shorter than a gnat's hiccup. No matter what Olga might tell him, I deduced it wouldn't be good, and it was easy to imagine a hairy nail keg drop-kicking me through a second-story window. Still, I was not the sort of person to be intimidated by childish threats, as I immediately demonstrated to an astonished Olga. In fact, in only my first three throws of the dice, I got out of med school, interned at a major hospital, and was making big bucks performing cardiovascular surgery.

Not only was the game boring, but it lasted slightly longer than the last ice age. By the time it ended, my mental faculties felt as if they had been stir-fried in molasses. I staggered off home and dropped immediately into bed.

The next morning I awoke with a jolt, realizing that somewhere in the fiasco with Olga I had mislaid my rifle. I left the house so fast the screen door twanged for a week. But the .22 was not to be found. It was as if it had slipped from my sweating palms the day before and disappeared down a gopher hole. My grief was monumental and has lingered even into the present day, causing me still to hold the entire medical profession in general distrust and responsible for the loss of my .22.

The following spring I found the rifle on a stack of fence posts, where it had wintered over. As a boy, I often read many articles that warned of the ills of failing to clean and oil a gun after each use, but never did I read an article warning against leaving a gun on a stack of fence posts all winter. You would think some shooting editor might have mentioned that at least once.

"So that's how my .22 got rusted and pitted," I told the burglar, who seemed on the verge of suffering an infarction of some sort. "Now, moving right along, this rather peculiar-looking rifle here is actually a .270. I restocked it myself with the arm from an old rocking chair and—"

The burglar held up a hand for me to cease. "Listen, pal," he said, "maybe I'll just take da TV after all. You can keep da guns."

Clearly, the man had been touched by my show of affection for the guns, which was what I had hoped for. Out of appreciation for his change of heart, I led him back to the living room, loaded him up with the TV, and even tried to warn him when he started out the wrong door. When the ruckus in the yard finally died down, I went back to bed.

"Is the burglar finished?" my wife asked sleepily.

"I'm afraid so," I said. "If the poor devil had had enough sense to drop the TV, he probably could have made it over the back fence before Felix got him. You know, having an attack cat isn't such a bad idea; but if these burglaries ever let up, we're going to have to start buying cat food for him."

Salami on Rye
and Hold
the Wild Gobo

"**D**id you know that cattails are good to eat?" my wife asked me one evening, looking up from the book she was reading.

"Who says?"

"Euell Gibbons."

"Well, Gibbons may know something about the Roman Empire, but he doesn't know a damn thing about cattails," I responded authoritatively. "They are not good to eat!"

"That was Gibbon who knew about the Roman Empire. Gibbons is an expert on wild foods."

Well, it just so happens, as I pointed out to Bun, that I too am an expert on wild foods. I was taught about them as a boy by my grandmother.

Few things were more dreaded in our house during my youth than Gram's announcement, "I think I'll go out to the woods and pick us a mess of wild greens for supper. Don't that sound good?"

"Mmmmmmm," Dad would say, because he hated to hurt Gram's feelings.

"Aagghhh!" my sister and I would say, because we detested Gram's wild greens. Then Dad would get us off in a corner and make some threats. He always referred to these threats as "a piece of advice."

"Let me give you two a piece of advice," he would say. "You eat your grandmother's greens without a word, and if she asks you how you like them, you smile and go 'mmmmmmm.' *Or else!*"

We would try to get him to be more specific about the "or else" so we could weigh the punishment against eating the greens, but he would stand pat on the vague and ominous threat.

The truth was Dad hated the greens as much as we did. He told my mother once that he would rather see the wolf crouched at the door than Gram coming through it with a mess of her wild greens. But he would never for the world let Gram think that they weren't practically his favorite food.

At supper he would be solemnly munching his way through the generous portion of wild greens to which he had masochistically helped himself, when Gram would ask, "How do you like the greens, Frank?"

Dad would look up and smile and go "mmmmmmm," but his eyes would be all wild and terrible. Then he would shoot my sister and me his "or else" look, and we would attack our own portions, which would be about the size of postage stamps but more than ample.

"And how do you children like the greens?" Gram would ask. We would first check out our glowering father, then smile weakly and go "mmm-*gag*-mmmmm."

I vividly recall the time Dad drew among his portion of the greens a particularly noxious sprout, its presence in the mess no doubt due to Gram's failing eyesight. (It was generally suspected that if a thing was vaguely green and appeared not to be moving under its own power, Gram picked it.)

Dad bit into the renegade sprout just after he had smiled and gone "mmmmmmm" in response to one of Gram's inquiries about the greens. (When he was eating her wild greens she could have asked him if he'd had a hard day, and he would have smiled and gone "mmmmmmm.") Suddenly, he stiffened in his chair and his fork clattered to the floor. "What is it?" Mom asked, thinking he was having an attack of some kind, and I guess he was. He stomped his foot several times, shook his head, swallowed mightily, and then drained his water glass in a single gulp.

Wiping his nose and eyes discreetly on his sleeve, he glanced over at Gram and offered the opinion, "Some of these greens have a powerful flavor."

Gram, oblivious of the preceding activity, peered at him over her spectacles. "Don't they, though! Try 'em with a little cinnamon. They taste even better that way."

I don't know about the cinnamon, but I could have tried them with Dutch Cleanser and they wouldn't have tasted any worse.

Gram was also a great believer in natural remedies for illness. Once when my sister was sick, or claiming to be, possibly because we were scheduled to have a mess of wild greens for supper, Gram concocted one of her folk medicines. The only ingredient that I can recall with any certainty was sap from a balsam tree in our yard. There was some yellow stuff, too, either sulfur or mustard powder, and I believe some water and molasses.

She boiled the mixture down to concentrate it, and then took a tablespoonful in to my sister, the very picture of infirmity as she lay in bed.

"Here, dear, take this," Gram said, pinching Trudy's cheeks to open her mouth, and pouring in the yellowish-brown substance. "It will have you up and around in no time."

Well, Gram was right about that. Ol' Trudy was up and around in one second, gasping, gagging, choking, knocking over furniture, and kicking walls. It was a miraculously quick cure and worthy of being written up in medical journals. And not only did the remedy cure childhood illnesses instantly, but it had wonderful preventive powers. In fact, neither Trudy nor I was ever sick again in all the rest of the time Gram stayed with us.

When I grew up and married, I thought wild greens were behind me once and for all. Then Bun read *Stalking the Wild Asparagus* by Euell Gibbons. Soon she was insisting that we stalk not only the wild asparagus, but the wild cattail, the wild milkweed, the wild burdock, the wild pokeweed, and a dozen other wild foods. "You never know when a knowledge of wild foods might come in handy," she would say ominously.

It wouldn't have been so bad if we could have done our stalking in the woods and swamps, but we lived in a city. One day as we walked along the sidewalk past a weedy vacant lot strewn with the rusting carcasses of dead cars, Bun suddenly gasped, "Wild gobo!"

Well, I scarcely jumped more than a foot in the air, which says something for my self-control, for I fully expected some hulking menace to be charging in our direction. "Where? Where?"

"There," Bun said, pointing to some weeds. "Wild gobo, also known as great burdock, *Arctium lappa*."

"*Arctium lappa* my clavicle," I snarled.

I hated stalking wild foods with Bun almost as much as I did eating them. (Bun, with tears welling: "You don't like my pokeweed ragout!" Me, smiling weakly: "Mmmmmmm!") The problem with stalking wild foods in the city was that they always grew on somebody else's property. There were two modes of operation open to us. We could sneak onto the lot, dig up or hack down some of the weeds, and then flee to the car for a fast getaway. Or we could ask permission of the property owner: "Sir, I wonder if you'd mind if I hacked off a bit of your wild gobo." It always seemed easier to me just to sneak onto the property without permission.

Through all of this I tried to explain to Bun how to interpret the terminology used in wild food books. For example, *edible* does not mean "good to eat." Edible means only that you won't flop over with your face in your plate when you take a bite of the stuff. *Choice* does not mean choice. It means only that if you feed the food to an unsuspecting dinner guest he won't chase you out of the house trying to plunge a table fork into your back.

"I don't believe it," Bun would say.

"It's true," I'd reply. "Listen, if the cattail was actually *good* to eat, they'd sell it in supermarkets for three dollars a pound. I rest my case."

I must admit that my experience with wild foods has not been all bad. Wild mushrooms are a case in point. I am a fungiphile of long standing, and devote countless hours searching for succulent morsels of the half-dozen varieties I know how to identify. Indeed, I owe it to the humble shaggymanes for once improving the general quality of my life, if not actually preserving my sanity.

Many years ago I had a friend named Stretch who worked nights at a warehouse. Apparently the job wasn't too difficult, because every night he found time to write half a dozen poems. After he got off work, in the morning, he would rush over to my house to read me his latest creations. While I ate breakfast, he would sit down at the table with me, refusing all offers of food and drink. Then he would say, "Oh, maybe I will have a cup of coffee, if it isn't too much bother." After a while he would add, "Say, that toast looks awfully good. Do you mind? Thanks. Please pass the jam." And a bit later: "Were you planning on eating both those strips of bacon?" And so on. Soon I would be at the stove frying him over-easy eggs and "a few hash browns, if you have some handy, and maybe three or four more strips of that bacon."

Now, Stretch was a fine fellow and good company, and I did not mind at all feeding him breakfast every morning. The problem was his poetry, which was of the Naturalistic school and leaned heavily on an *S* alliteration: "Sad, sorrow-sunk survivors of a sadistic society, saturated with strong, stiff stench of stifling strife . . ." In short, it was not poetry to eat breakfast by. Every morning I would go off to work in a somber, Naturalistic mood and throughout the day would find myself saying such things to my fellow workers as, "Sara, send Sally for six or so sheets of seven-cent stamps."

One day walking home from work I spotted a nice patch of shaggymane mushrooms growing on a lawn and, with the stealth known only to foragers of wild food in an urban setting, quickly filled my hat with them.

The next morning I cooked up the mess of mushrooms and was just sitting down to enjoy them when Stretch bounded through the door, the night's output of poems clutched in his hand.

"Breakfast, Stretch?" I asked as he sat down at the table and began arranging his works for the reading.

"No, nothing for me, thanks. This first poem I titled 'Slime.' I think you will like it. Oh, maybe I will have a cup of coffee, if it's not too much bother."

Then Stretch saw the dish of shaggymanes. "What's that?"

"Mushrooms."

"Mind if I try them?"

"Be my guest," I said, sliding the dish over and handing him a fork.

"Hey, these are delicious!" Stretch exclaimed and continued to fork in my shaggymanes between stanzas of "Slime." Upon completion of the reading, he asked, "How did you like it?"

"Great," I said. "How did you like the mushrooms?"

Stretch ran his finger around the dish and licked the juice off of it appreciatively. "Just the best thing I ever ate, that's all," he said. "What kind were they?"

"Beats me," I said.

"You don't *know?*" he said, staring at his licked finger as if it were a coral snake.

"I found them growing in the yard and thought they looked good enough to eat," I said.

Stretch looked around wildly. "But you're not supposed to do that!"

"Why not?" I said. "It's my yard, I can pick mushrooms in it if I want."

"No, that's not . . . I mean . . . look, I got to go!"

Since my eyes were in the middle of a blink at the time, I didn't see Stretch leave, but I noted that the swiftness of his departure had sent the poems floating about the kitchen like autumn leaves in a brisk wind. While conjecturing to myself about Stretch's intended destination, I gathered up the poems and placed them neatly on the shelf to return to him the next time he stopped by to give me readings at breakfast. The poems gathered dust there for many months, and now I'm not sure what happened to them. I suppose they weren't such bad poems either, particularly if you're unusually fond of the S sound.

Two-Man-Tent Fever

Fenton Quagmire was telling me recently about the weekend he had just suffered through at his lakeside retreat.

"Rained the whole time, and I didn't get outside once," he said. "By Sunday I had a case of the cabin fever like you wouldn't believe!"

Wouldn't believe? Why, I could barely keep from doubling over in a paroxysm of mirth!

I happen to know that Quagmire's "cabin" is a three-bedroom, shag-carpeted, TV-ed, and hot-tubbed villa overlooking a stretch of sandy beach that sells per linear foot at the same rate as strung pearls. Obviously, what Quagmire had experienced was nothing more than *villa fever*, which compares to cabin fever as the sniffles to double pneumonia.

True cabin fever requires a true cabin—four buckling walls, a leaky roof, a warped floor, a door, and a few windows. Furnishings consist of something less than the bare necessities. Wall decorations, while permitted, should not be such as to arouse any visual interest whatsoever. (The old Great Northern Railroad calendar with the mountain goat on it is about right.) A wood stove, preferably one made from a steel barrel, provides the heat, and also the only excitement, when its rusty tin pipe sets fire to the roof. That's your basic true cabin.

When I was six, we lived for a year in just such a cabin. My father speculated that it had been built by a man who didn't know his adz from his elbow, or words to that effect. The shake roof looked as if it had been dealt out by an inebriated poker player during a sneezing fit. Proper alignment of one log over another was so rare as to suggest coincidence, if not divine intervention. The man who rented the cabin to us, apparently a buff of local history, boasted that it had been built toward the end of the last century. "Which end?" Dad asked him.

Within a short while after we moved in, Dad had the cabin whipped into shape, a shape that might now be regarded as unfit for human habitation but which in those days would generally have been thought of as unfit for human habitation. After hammering in the last nail, Dad unscrewed the cap from a quart of his home brew, took a deep swig, and told my mother, "This is as good as it gets!" I have, of course, re-created the quote, but it captures the proper note of pessimism.

One might suppose that a family of four would be miserable living in a tiny, sagging log cabin in the middle of an Idaho wilderness, and one would be right. My mother and sister accepted our situation philosophically and cried only on alternate days. Dad arose early each morning and went off in search of "suitable work," by which he meant work that paid anything at all. I spent my time morosely digging away at the chinking between the logs, not realizing that the resulting cracks would let all the cold out.

One day in the middle of January, Mom looked up from her bowl of gruel at breakfast, as we jokingly referred to it, and announced, "Well, we've finally hit rock bottom. Things just can't get any worse." We soon discovered that Mom lacked the gift of prophecy.

Within hours, the mercury was rattling about like a dried pea in the bulb of the thermometer, and the wind came blasting out of the north. Strangely, Dad seemed delighted by the onset of a blizzard. Even now, four decades later, I can still see him bending over, rubbing a hole in the window frost with his fist and peering out at the billowing snow.

"Let her blow!" he shouted. "We've got plenty of firewood and enough grub to last until spring if we have to! By gosh, we'll just make some fudge, pop corn, and play Monopoly until she blows herself out! It'll be like a little adventure, like we're shipwrecked!"

The rest of the family was instantly perked up by his enthusiasm and defiance of the blizzard. Mom started making fudge and popping corn, while my sister and I rushed to set up the Monopoly game.

The blizzard lasted nearly two weeks, give or take a century. By the third day my sister and I were forbidden even to mention Monopoly, fudge, or popcorn. And Dad no longer regarded the blizzard as a little adventure.

"Why are you making that noise with your nose?" he would snarl at me.

"I'm just breathing."

"Well, stop it!"

"Whose idea was that calendar?" he'd snap at my mother.

"What's wrong with it, dear?"

"That stupid mountain goat watches every move I make, that's what! Look how its eyes follow me!"

A day or two later, as Dad himself admitted at the time, he became irritable.

Shortly after that, he came down with cabin fever.

Spending several days trapped in close quarters with a person who had cabin fever toughened me up a lot psychologically. A couple of years later, when I saw the movie *Frankenstein Meets the Wolf Man*, I thought it was a comedy. At the peak of his cabin fever, Dad could have played both leads in the film simultaneously and sent audiences screaming into the streets.

The only good thing about cabin fever is that it vanishes the instant the victim is released from enforced confinement. When the county snowplow finally opened the road and came rumbling into our yard, Dad strolled out to greet and thank the driver.

"Snowed in fer a spell, weren't ya?" the driver said. "Bet you got yerself a good case of the cabin fever."

"Naw," Dad said. "It wasn't bad. We just made fudge and popped corn and played a few games of Monop . . . Monop . . . played a few games."

"Well, you certainly seem normal enough," the driver said. Then he pointed to Mom, Sis, and me. "That your family?"

It seemed like an odd question, but I suppose the driver wondered why a normal man like my father would have a family consisting of three white-haired gnomes.

There are numerous kinds of fever brought on by

the boredom of enforced confinement over long periods. I myself have contracted some of the lesser strains—coldwater-flat fever, mobile-home fever, and split-level fever, to name but a few. I have never been able to afford the more exotic and expensive fevers, like those of my wealthy friend Quagmire. In addition to his villa fever, he will occasionally run a continent fever, one of the symptoms of which is the sensation that the Atlantic and Pacific coastlines are closing in on him. The treatment, as I understand it, is to take two aspirin and a Caribbean cruise.

Of all such fevers, by far the most deadly is two-man-tent fever, which, in its severity, surpasses even the cabin variety.

I had the opportunity of studying two-man-tent fever close-up a few years ago, when Parker Whitney and I spent nearly twenty hours in his tiny tent waiting for a storm to blow over. Parker is a calm, quiet chap normally, and it was terrible to see him go to pieces the way he did, after the fever overtook him.

For a while, during the first few hours of the storm, we were entertained by the prospect that we might momentarily be using the tent as a hang glider. After the wind died down to a modest gale, we were able to devote our whole attention to the rippling of the orange ripstop nylon that enveloped us. Fascinating as this was, its power to distract was limited to a few hours. By then, I was formulating a geological theory that a major earth fault lay directly beneath, and crossed at right angles to, my half-inch Ensolite pad. While several of my more adventuresome vertebrae were testing this theory, I gradually became aware that Parker was beginning to exhibit certain signs of neurotic behavior.

"I hate to ask this, old chap," I said, kindly enough, "but would you mind not chewing that gum quite so loud?"

Parker replied with uncharacteristic snappishness. "For the fourteenth time, I'm not chewing gum!"

Mild hallucination is one of the early symptoms of two-man-tent fever. Not only did Parker fail to realize that he was chomping and popping his gum in a hideous manner, but he clearly was of the impression that I had mentioned the matter to him numerous times previously. Since hallucinations do not yield readily to logical argument, I thought that confronting him with the empirical evidence might work. Unfortunately, Parker was now in the grip of paranoia and responded to my effort by shouting out that I had "gone mad." I suppose he was referring to the manner in which I had grabbed him by the nose and chin and forced his mouth open, a maneuver that proved ineffective, since he had somehow managed to hide the gum from my vision and probing thumb, possibly by lodging it behind his tonsils. Such deception, I might add, is not at all unusual among victims of two-man-tent fever.

Parker remained quiet for some time, although I could tell from the look in his eyes that the paranoia was tightening its hold on him, and I began to wonder if my life might not be in danger. I warned him not to try anything.

"Why don't you get some sleep?" Parker replied. "Just try to get some sleep!"

"Ha!" I said, not without a trace of sarcasm. "Do you really think I'm going to fall for that old one?"

I twisted around in my bag and propped up on an elbow so I could watch Parker more closely. It was easy to see that the two-man-tent fever was taking its toll on him. He was pale and trembling, and stared back at me with wide, unblinking eyes. He looked pitiful, even though posing no less a threat to my life.

Then, as if our situation were not perilous enough already, I noticed that Parker had dandruff. Under normal circumstances, I can take dandruff or leave it alone, but not in a two-man tent. It wasn't the unsightly appearance of the dandruff that bothered me, but the little *plip plip plip* sounds it made falling on his sleeping bag. I soon deduced that Parker had contrived this irritation for the sole purpose of annoying me, a sort of Chinese dandruff torture, although I hadn't realized until then that Parker was Chinese. Informing him that I was on to his little game, I told Parker to get his dandruff under control or suffer the consequences. Not surprisingly, he denied any knowledge of his dandruff or its activities. I therefore retaliated by doing my impression of Richard Widmark's maniacal laugh every time I heard a *plip*. Parker countered by doing his impression of a man paralyzed by fear. It wasn't that good, as impressions go, but I withheld criticism of the poor devil's performance, since it seemed to take his mind off the fever.

At the first break in the storm, Parker shot out of the tent, stuffed his gear into his pack, and took off down the trail, leaving me with the chore of folding up the tent and policing camp. Before I was finished, a ranger came riding up the trail on a horse. We exchanged pleasantries, and I asked him if he had happened to pass my partner on the trail.

"I don't know," he said. "Is he a white-haired gnome?"

Fish Poles, and Other Useful Terminology

I have long held the opinion that a person should know the jargon of any activity in which he professes some expertise. A writer, for example, should not refer to quotation marks as "those itty-bitty ears." It is unsettling to hear the carpenter you have just hired refer to his hammer as "a pounder." A mechanic tinkering in the innards of your car arouses anxiety by speaking of a pair of pliers as his "squeezer." Similarly, it would be disconcerting to have a doctor tell you he had detected an irregularity in your "thingamajig." (If you're like me, you're composed almost entirely of thingamajigs, some of which you value a good deal more than others.) Ignorance of proper terminology often leads to confusion, alarm, and panic, especially when one talks about the sport of fishing.

I recently met a man and his son out bass fishing. The father was making superb casts with what was obviously a new rod.

"Is that a boron you've got there?" I asked.

The man turned and looked at his son. "Well, he ain't too bright, that's for sure," he said.

Here was a case where a man had mastered the art of fishing, but had failed to keep up on recent nomenclature. I could hardly blame him. I now spend so much time learning all the new fishing terms that I scarcely have time to fish.

Non-anglers think fishing is easy. Well, just let them spend a day poring over one of the new fishing catalogs and memorizing the terms. One 1982 catalog, for example, contains such terms and phrases as "fiberglass integrated with unidirectional graphite," "silicone carbide guides with diamond polished silicone carbide guide rings," "Uni bent butt," that sort of thing. I'm just lucky I didn't ask the man fishing with his son if he had a Uni bent butt. I might have come home with a Uni bent head.

Consider just a few of the terms you now must learn in order to go out and catch a few bass: *structure, isolated structure, sanctuary, stragglers, breakline, suspended fish, pattern, holding area, riprap, point, scatter point, contact point, cheater hook, buzz bait, Texas rig, crank bait, triggering, flippin', pH, jig and pig, spinnerbait, fly 'n' rind.* The aerospace industry requires less technical jargon than the average bass fisherman.

When I was a youngster, my friends and I could get by on fewer than a dozen fishing terms. No doubt we could have expanded our angling vocabulary by going to the county library and checking out a book on fishing techniques. The problem was that if one of the gang showed up at the library to check out a book, Miss Phelps, the librarian, might have suffered a heart attack on the spot. Enlarging our fishing vocabularies didn't seem worth the risk of taking a life. We chose to get by on the few fishing terms we knew.

Although our fishing terminology was limited, it was not without its own peculiar complexity. Take the word *keeper* for example. The first fish you caught was always a "keeper." This was not the result of outrageous coincidence, but of definition. The first fish was interpreted as a "keeper" merely by having a mouth big enough to stretch over the barb of a hook.

There were several advantages to this definition of *keeper* applying to the first fish. Suppose the first fish you caught during the day was also the only fish, and you had released it. That would mean you would have to go home *skunked,* an angling term every bit as significant then as it is today. Calling the first fish a "keeper" often prevented the emotional damage which resulted from going home "skunked."

Furthermore, if someone later asked you if you had caught any fish, you could reply, in reference to a fish no longer than a pocketknife, "Just one keeper." The phrase *just one keeper* implied, of course, that you had caught and released numerous *small* fish, thereby contributing to one's reputation as a "sportsman."

If the first fish was particularly small, it did not always remain a "keeper." A larger fish, when caught, became a "keeper" and the small first fish became a *badly hooked* one. You always explained, with a note of regret in your voice, that you had kept the "badly hooked" fish because it would have "died anyway." Proper fishing terminology even in the time of my youth was extremely important, both socially and psychologically.

Although some of our terms might seem simple by

today's standards, they were not without their subtle shades of meaning. Take the word *mess* for instance, which was the word used to denote your catch while telling someone about your day of fishing. *Mess* used without modifiers usually meant two fish—a "keeper" and a "badly hooked." A *small mess* referred to a single "keeper." A *nice mess* meant three fish, excluding any "badly hooked." Any number of fish over three was, naturally, a *big mess.* To ask for specific numbers was considered rude when someone told you he had caught a "big mess" of fish.

Today, the phrase *a mess of fish* is seldom heard, probably because anyone uttering it would instantly be identifying himself as a fish glutton. Quantity of the catch is now always referred to by specific numbers, although a certain element of deception is still retained. An angler who has spent twelve hours flailing a trout stream, and managed to land a total of three fish, responds to a question about the number of fish caught by saying "I only *kept* three." If asked exactly how many he caught and released, he will be overcome by a coughing fit and have to rush from the room. Now, as always, it is considered poor form to lie about the number of fish caught, unless, of course, the angler has not mastered the technique of the coughing fit.

It took me fifteen minutes the other day to memorize the name of my new casting rod, and I've already forgotten it. When I was younger, we didn't have to memorize the names of our rods because we didn't have any. We had what were called "fish poles." Even now, after nearly forty years, I will still occasionally refer to a three-hundred-dollar custom-built fly rod as a "fish pole."

"That's a nice fish pole you've got there," I'll say to the owner of the rod.

He will go white in the face, shudder, twitch, gurgle, clench his hands, and lurch toward me. "Wha-what d-did you s-say? F-fish pole? FISH POLE! Y-you called my three-hundred-dollar rod a FISH POLE?"

I will back away, hands raised to fend him off, and explain that I have never shaken a bad habit picked up in my childhood.

Fish pole, in the old days, was a generic term for any elongated instrument intended for the purpose of propelling hook, line, sinker, and worm in the general direction of fish-holding water, and then wrenching an unlucky fish to the bank with as little fuss as possible. Some fish poles were made from cedar trees that had been rejected as too short or too slender for use as telephone poles. A few fortunate kids owned metal telescoping fish poles. My first fish pole was a single-piece, stiff metal tube about six feet long. There was a wire that could be pulled out of the tip if you wanted "action." I never pulled the wire out. Action, in my fishing circles, was not considered a desirable characteristic in a fish pole. It merely complicated the process of wrenching the fish from the water, or *landing it.*

Landing, by the way, consisted of whipping the fish in a long, high arc over your head and into the branches of a tree, which you usually had to climb in order to disengage both line and fish. Sometimes the fish would come off the line right at the peak of the arc and whiz away toward the state line like a stone loosed from a sling. These fish were later referred to as "badly hooked."

Forked stick is a term seldom heard among anglers nowadays, which is too bad, because the forked stick once served to enrich both fishing and conversations about fishing.

"I prefer the forked stick to a creel for carrying fish," a kid would say. "The creel is too bulky and keeps catching on brush. It gets in your way when you're casting, too. Most creels are too small for a really big fish anyway. Give me a forked stick to a creel any time." This statement actually meant "Give me a forked stick any time until someone gives me a creel. Then I'll prefer a creel."

There was much discussion about the kind of tree or bush that produced the best forked sticks for carrying fish. In theory, the way you selected a forked stick was to seek out a good specimen from the preferred species of bush or tree, cut it off with your pocketknife, and neatly trim it to appropriate and aesthetically pleasing dimensions. Ideally, there would be a fork at both ends, one to keep the fish from sliding off and the other to be hooked under your belt, thus freeing both hands for the business of catching fish.

The theory of the forked stick didn't work out in practice, because the kid never even thought about cutting a forked stick until he had caught his first fish. To cut a forked stick prior to catching a fish would have been presumptuous and probably bad luck to boot. (Also, few things look more ridiculous than an angler walking around with an empty forked stick.) Once a fish had been caught, the youngster, in his excitement, would instantly forget the aesthetically pleasing proportions prescribed for the forked stick. He would twist off the nearest branch with a fork on it, gnaw away any obstructing foliage with his teeth, thread the fish onto it, and get back to his fishing. When you were catching fish, you didn't have time to mess with aesthetics.

The forked stick contributed much excitement to our fishing. Since a double-forked branch or willow was almost never available when needed, the forked stick could not be hooked under your belt but had to be laid down somewhere while you fished. Once or twice every hour, a panicky search would begin for a string of fish left on a log or rock "just around that last bend." Approximately thirty percent of your fishing time was spent trying to catch fish and seventy percent looking for fish you had already caught.

Thus, the term *forked stick* denoted not merely a device for carrying your catch, but a whole mode of fishing that the boy who grows up owning a creel can never come to know or appreciate. He should consider himself damn lucky for it, too.

There were a few other terms that filled out our fishing vocabulary. *Game warden* is one that comes to mind. I don't know if any state still has game wardens. Most have *Wildlife Conservation Officers* or persons of similar sterile title to enforce fishing regulations. Somehow it doesn't seem to me that "Wildlife Conservation Officer" has the same power to jolt a boy's nervous system as does "game warden." How well I remember a fishing pal once exclaiming, "Geez, here comes the *game warden!*" We jerked our lines from the creek, sprinted up the side of a steep, brush-covered hill, threw our fish poles and forked sticks under a log, and tore off across the countryside. And we hadn't even been violating any of the fishing regulations. The term *game warden* just had that sort of effect on you.

There is at least one indication that many terms and phrases closely associated with fishing may soon be made obsolete. A new reel on the market is reputed to virtually eliminate backlash, that wonderfully intricate snarl of line that has served to enrich the vocabularies of anglers ever since reels were invented. It seems likely the eradication of backlash could mean the end of such colorful expressions as *bleeping bleep of a bleep bleep.* Truly, the language of fishing will be the less for the absence of backlash.

And it's about time, if you ask me.

The Man Who Notices Things

Fenton Quagmire has this irritating habit—he notices things. Even when we were kids, Fenton noticed things.

Our fourth-grade teacher, Mrs. Terwilliger, was keen on noticing things herself. "All right, class," she'd say, "who noticed anything different about our room today? Pat?"

"There's a picture of George Washington on the wall?" I'd try hopefully.

"That picture' has been there ever since they built the school! Now, Eugene, do you notice anything different about the room?"

"Nope."

"Lester?"

"Unh-unh."

One by one, Mrs. Terwilliger would call out the names of the boys in the class and ask if they noticed anything different about the room. They would reply with negative grunts, wild guesses, and looks of total befuddlement. (She never called on any of the girls, of course, since it is well known that girls notice things.) Finally, the teacher would get to Quagmire, who would have been waving his hand in the air and snapping his fingers for attention. "All right now, Fenton, I want you to tell these dunces what's different about the room today."

Quagmire would then point out some piddling detail, such as that the wall to the cloakroom had been removed, or all the seats were facing in a different direction, or Mrs. Terwilliger was dressed up like Woody Woodpecker. We dunces would emerge from our lethargy long enough to express our amazement that we had failed to notice the thing, whatever it was, and would whisper vows among ourselves to make life miserable for Quagmire at the next recess.

The casual observer might suppose that the rest of us boys enjoyed tormenting Quagmire, and we were frequently hauled into the principal's office to face such charges. The truth was, it was Quagmire who tormented the rest of us. I remember, for example, a championship softball game in which we were ahead by one run in the ninth inning, and the opposing team, with two outs, had the bases loaded. An easy fly ball was batted out to Quagmire in center field. The ball bounced alongside him and disappeared into a weed patch. He was on his hands and knees staring at the ground. Cries of rage and anguish went up from the rest of our team.

"Hey, guys," Quagmire shouted. "Guess what I just noticed out here—a four-leaf clover!" In his peculiar innocence, he assumed that the reason his teammates were converging on him so rapidly was to satisfy a life-long curiosity about four-leaf clovers.

I saw that it was up to me to save him. In the musical chairs of childhood relationships, Quagmire was from time to time my best friend, and this was one of those times. The code back then required that you do whatever you could to save your best friend, so I immediately took defensive action on his behalf. "Run, Quagmire, run!" I shouted. "But first, grab that four-leaf clover, because you're gonna need all the luck you can get!"

Sometimes I wasn't able to save Quagmire from the violence he called down upon himself. Once, he and I went fishing together on the opening day of trout season. I was still in the grip of first-cast-of-the-season jitters as we waded through some tall grass on the way to our favorite fishing hole. Suddenly, Quagmire pointed at my feet and shouted, "Look out!"

In response, I raised both knees up alongside my ears, then did some aerial gymnastics that would have shamed a Nadia Comaneci.

"What?" I yelled, still treading air. *"What is it?"*

"Why, didn't you notice these little globs of foam on the grass?" said Quagmire. "You nearly stepped on them. See, they look like spit, and there's a little bug inside each glob. I'll bet these little bugs make spit houses for themselves. If you'll notice, right here is a *glug arf ugh lo mawf froat!"*

Bug-spit houses! It was just lucky for Quagmire that my hands were too weak at age ten to effectively strangle a person. Nevertheless, it was some years before he again noticed anything in close proximity to my feet.

My friend and mentor, the old woodsman Rancid Crabtree, could not abide Quagmire. Once when Fenton and I were in high school, I suggested to Rancid that we take him hunting with us.

"No! No! No!" yelled Rancid. "He ain't goin' huntin' with us, an' thet's final! Ah cain't stand the way thet boy is all the time noticin' stuff what ain't even worth bein' noticed!"

"Oh, c'mon, Rancid," I urged. "Fenton doesn't have anybody else to hunt with."

"Waall, shoot!" Rancid said. "Mebby this one time. But you tell him we're goin' huntin' and not just out noticin' thangs. You got it?"

"Right."

I had a little talk with Quagmire, and he promised he would try not to notice anything on our hunting trip. He did try, too, I'm sure of that.

Driving up into the mountains on our hunt, Quagmire could scarcely contain himself. He would glance out the window and then swivel his head around. "Say, did you . . ." he'd start to say. I'd elbow him in the ribs and he'd shut up.

"What's thet?" Rancid would say, glaring. Quagmire's eyes would be wild with excitement over what he had just noticed.

"Nothing," he'd say.

Then Quagmire started studying the dashboard on Rancid's old truck as we bounced along. "Pardon me for mentioning this, Mr. Crabtree, but I noti—" I jammed my elbow into his ribs. "B-but . . . !" he sputtered. I shook my head at him. From then on, the drive was peaceful, and if Quagmire noticed anything else, he had the good sense not to mention it.

A couple of hours later we were trying to catch up with a herd of mule deer we had jumped earlier. Quagmire was making a sweep around the mountain above us, while Rancid and I, having about given up hope of ever catching sight of the mule deer again, rested at the foot of a high cliff. Rancid was stoking his lip with tobacco, when Quagmire appeared at the top of the cliff, frantically signaling to us.

"Gol-dang!" whispered Rancid. "The boy's seen the herd! Ah always said he warn't a bad feller! Ah guess the only thang we can do is climb the cliff."

"Gee," I whispered back. "It's awfully steep. I don't think we can climb clear to the top."

"Shore we can!" Rancid hissed.

Halfway up the cliff, Rancid spat his tobacco out into space. "Ah got some bad news fer ya," he said to me.

"What's that?" I asked.

"Ah don't thank we can make it all the way to the top," he grunted, his clawed fingers digging into a vertical slab of granite. "But thet ain't the bad news."

"Well," I gasped, "what's the bad news?"

"Ah don't thank we can climb back down nuther!"

I considered Rancid's assessment of our predicament much too optimistic. Fortunately, at that moment I discovered an inch-wide ledge that angled right up under the overhang that was covered with wet moss. "This way, Rancid," I said. "I see a way out." And sure enough, scraped, battered, and bruised, the two of us soon scrambled over the lip of the cliff.

"Dang," Rancid said, rubbing his knee as we looked around for Quagmire. "Ah shore wouldn't hev wore maw good pants iffen Ah'd know'd we was gonna climb thet cliff today."

"Tear 'em, did you?"

"No. Now, whar in tarnation is thet Quagmire?"

Presently, we saw him crouched behind some brush, signaling to us. Unslinging our rifles, we hustled over in a walking crouch, being careful not to make any sound that would spook the deer.

"Whar is they, Fenton?" Rancid whispered, peering around over the top of the brush.

"This is fantastic!" Quagmire said. "Look at these rocks here. I was just walking along when I noticed them. See how round they are? Why, they're river rocks! What are river rocks doing this far up on the side of a mountain? Do you know what this means?"

"Yup," growled Rancid. "It means, Quagmire, thet whan you pick up one of them rocks thar better be a herd of deer under it!"

The river rocks weren't even the worst part of our day. When we got back to Rancid's truck, it wouldn't start. "That's what I tried to tell you, Mr. Crabtree," Quagmire said. "I noticed on the way up here that your gas gauge was on empty."

Rancid leaned his head on the steering wheel. I didn't know whether he was crying or just counting to ten.

Middle age hasn't diminished Quagmire's obsession with noticing things. His hair is gray now, his face eroded by time and weather, but still the bright little eyes relentlessly ferret out things to notice. I dread having Quagmire come in the house when he picks me up to go fishing.

"I notice you got a new hairdo," he says to my wife. "Looks nice."

"Why, thank you," Bun says, adding, "I'm glad somebody noticed."

"My gosh, you did get a new hairdo," I exclaim. "When did you change from the bouffant?"

"Nineteen sixty-five."

"Oh."

Meanwhile, Quagmire has found something else to notice.

"What happened to your other goldfish?" he asks.

"It died last summer," Bun says.

"When did we get goldfish?" I inquire.

"I see you painted your living room blue," says Quagmire.

"You did?" I say to Bun. "Heck, I liked the brown."

"The brown was four colors ago," snarls Bun.

And so it goes. Needless to say, Quagmire is very popular with women, who seem to have a certain irrational regard for men who have a compulsion to notice trifling details. "Why can't you be more like Fenton?" Bun wails at me. "You never notice anything!"

Well, that's certainly not true, as I informed Bun in no uncertain terms. It's that I'm selective about what I notice. I don't just go around noticing indiscriminately, for pete's sake!

I recently spent three days hiking alone through the Cabinet Range of the Rocky Mountains, and Bun would have been amazed at all the things I noticed.

I noticed that the trails were a good deal steeper this year than last. This was no doubt the result of some foolishness on the part of the U.S. Forest Service. When I got back home, I fired off a letter to the USFS and told them to leave the trails alone—they're steep enough!

I noticed the nights are darker when you're alone in the mountains than when you have company. Scientists should investigate this phenomenon; it might be something the CIA could make use of.

I noticed, after a couple of hours of staring out into the abnormal darkness, that there was a hard, knobby object under my Ensolite pad, no doubt a seed dropped by a careless ant.

I noticed a mosquito, and marveled that a creature so small could be so enormously complex, and still could find nothing better to do with himself than walking around in my ear singing light opera.

I noticed an ant crawling up my leg, probably the same careless chap who had dropped the walnut that was under my Ensolite pad.

I noticed far off down in the valley the sound of a large, clawed foot pressing into moss.

I noticed that I didn't have a gun with me, and wondered if there was a tool on my Swiss Army knife with which to fend off a grizzly. Maybe the corkscrew. I imagined the headline in the newspaper: "Grizzly Corkscrewed by Lone Hiker."

I noticed that the ant had been joined by some friends and relatives. They were probably helping him look for his baseball.

I noticed the distant whistle of a train, and wished I was in the lounge car exchanging dry jokes and drier martinis with traveling salesmen.

I noticed that it was only a cold, slimy sleeping bag drawstring slithering across my neck, but not until I had killed it with a blow from my hiking boot. Should have waited until it was off my neck, though.

I noticed that the sound of the large, clawed foot was right next to me, and the beast was making an assault on my jerky bag! One usually doesn't find chipmunks with such large, clawed feet. He was a cheeky fellow, too. The sight of a man feinting wildly at him with a Swiss Army knife corkscrew scarcely fazed him.

I did enough noticing on that outing to give me my fill of it, and I haven't noticed anything since. A dog could ride past me on a unicycle smoking a cigar and doing an impression of Groucho Marx, and I wouldn't notice.

The first person I ran into on my return from the mountains was Quagmire. "That must have been quite a trip," he said. "I notice that you've lost fifteen pounds."

Ha! Quagmire isn't as perceptive as he likes to think. I hadn't lost an ounce over ten pounds!

The Elk Trappers

My wife and I were but a few years out of college and already surrounded by babies of our own making—a simple, inexpensive hobby that had somehow gotten out of hand. At the time, I was writing for all the big-name, high-paying national magazines. Unfortunately, they never bought anything I wrote. I did sell an occasional article to newspapers and regional magazines, but payment from these publications was small and slow in coming, often requiring that I go into the office to bend the editor's ear and sometimes his Adam's apple.

During my best year as a free-lance writer, our standard of living hovered constantly near the poverty level but was never quite high enough for us to qualify as poor. Bun's hopes and dreams had diminished in both number and magnitude since our marriage, and she now spoke wistfully of the day when we might move into a quaint little hovel of our very own. She was a marvelously inventive cook, however, and no matter how little food we might have, she was always able to come up with a delicious dish of some sort. One of my favorites was her Boston Baked Bean, which she served on holidays. I am probably the only person in the world who knows how to carve a bean properly. We used to tell the children it was a small turkey. "Who wants white meat?" I would ask.

After a while, our situation became so bad that even the surly henchmen from the collection agency stopped coming around, possibly because I kept bumming small loans off of them. Finally, I decided to commit the writer's ultimate act of despair, even though my own personal religion forbade such a drastic measure. Still, it seemed like the only way out of my predicament: I'd have to take a regular job.

In a disgustingly short time, I landed a position with a local television station as a reporter/photographer in the news department. It was dreadful. As I signed the W2 form, my whole life flashed before my eyes. Bun, however, was elated when I told her.

"Wonderful!" she cried. "We should celebrate! I'll go pop us a corn! What do you want to drink?"

"A schooner of tap," I said. "I've cultivated a taste for chlorine."

Right from the start, I did not get along with the news director at the station. He was a tough, burly individual, with a face like a fist and a temper shorter than a snake's inseam. His name was Pat Hooper. It was a simple enough name but for some reason I constantly messed up its pronunciation, particularly when we were doing a "live" show and I was supposed to say, "Now, back to Pat Hooper!"

"You idiot!" he would scream at me after the show. "You did it again!"

"Calm down, calm down," I'd say. "Now, just tell me nicely and quietly what it was I did wrong. After all, I'm still learning the business, Hat."

There were other problems. One time, rushing off to do an interview, I set one of the station's portable sound cameras on top of the news car while I loaded some other equipment. The next place I saw the camera was in my rearview mirror, bounding along behind my speeding car like a dog chasing after the family sedan.

Then there was the foggy night I called into the station from a pay phone on the outskirts of town. Hat himself answered.

"Boy, I never thought I'd be happy to hear your voice," he shouted over the phone. "The two-way radio in your news car must have conked out, huh? We've been trying to reach you for an hour. Anyway, we heard from the cops that some fool just drove his car into Mamford Lake! Drove right down the boat-launch ramp! And get this—*har, har!*—he told the cops he thought the lake was just a big puddle! Oh, *harharharheeeee!* Let me catch my breath! Okay, now here's what I want you to do. Get out to Mamford Lake as quick as you can and shoot some film and try to get an interview with the guy. It'll make a heck of a hilarious story for the late news!"

I waited until the news director's giggles had died down. "Listen, Hat, I'm already out at Mamford Lake, and I can tell you right now you're not going to find the story all that hilarious."

Probably the thing I hated most about being a television reporter was having to listen to a grown man sob so often.

Hat and I had got off to a bad start and our relationship had steadily deteriorated. After about a year, there was even some evidence that the news director had taken a personal dislike to me. Oh, there was nothing major, just little things I noticed, like the way he would slap at me if I passed too near his desk. I decided to confront him face to face and get the matter out in the open where we could deal with it like two mature adults.

During a quiet moment in the news room, I said, "Hat, there's something bothering you. I get the distinct impression that you are harboring some ill feelings toward me. Let's talk about it, what say, fella?"

"*Get this maniac away from me!*" Hat screamed to nobody in particular.

"Now right there is a good example of what I mean," I said. "Look, if I upset you so much, why don't you just go ahead and terminate me?"

"I might just do that," Hat replied. "Let's see, with time off for good behavior I'd be back on the streets in five years."

Then he sank back in his swivel chair and started doing his impression of a dog chewing hot pitch. Once he started acting silly like that, trying to converse with him in an intelligent manner was hopeless.

I was oddly upset over this little exchange with Hat. Indeed, it seemed likely that he was thinking of firing me. Never before had I worked at a job where I had even the slightest fear of being fired. (Usually, the news came as a total surprise.) What I needed, I knew, was a big story, something that would change Hat's opinion of me as a television reporter. I needed something with human interest, something with animals in it, big animals, wild animals, something with danger and courage and conflict, something with brave, dedicated men risking all to extend the horizons of human knowledge! And I knew of just such a story—The Elk Trappers!

A game biologist had recently told me about an elk-migration study being conducted in a wilderness area of a nearby state. Two men had been hired to trap— that's right, *trap*—elk. Once the elk were trapped, they were adorned with various paraphernalia for future tracking and identification on their travels about the mountains.

I could hardly wait to tell Hat about my story idea.

"What?" he said. "Elk trapping? Nonsense! What kind of stuff are you trying to pull on me now?"

"I'm not kidding, Hat," I said. "It'll make great film. Of course, I'll have to be away from the station for a whole week but. . . ."

"A whole week? You've got to stop reading my mind. I was just sitting here wondering when a good story on elk trapping might turn up!"

A few days later I was flailing my old sedan over a route that the U.S. Forest Service cartographer had designated with two parallel dotted lines. Only too late did I discover that the dots represented mountain goat tracks, the cartographer apparently having turned up some evidence that a mountain goat had managed to explore the region in rather aimless fashion sometime in the previous century. I could not help but agree that the goat's achievement had been heroic, but why the cartographer should choose to commemorate it with dots was beyond comprehension. A simple skull-and-crossbones with horns would have sufficed.

At long last I spotted the elk trappers' camp nestled

in a grove of cedars near the foot of a precipice, the upper rim of which my vehicle was momentarily teetering upon. Having come this far, I was not about to turn back simply because of a near-perpendicular descent of a few hundred feet. Shifting my weight, I tilted the car forward. Judges of free-fall events probably would have disqualified me on the technicality that my car's tires occasionally brushed protruding rocks on the drop. The wall of the precipice swooped outward in a curve similar to that of a playground slide, and I was able to regain control of the vehicle in sufficient time to bring it to a screeching stop a good six inches from the tent of the elk trappers. In fact for several moments after the stop, I continued to screech, as did the elk trappers, who had shot from the tent with a suddenness that caused me to wonder if the two of them might not have been sitting in some kind of spring-loaded catapult, awaiting my arrival.

Mort and Wally, as I'll call the trappers, turned out to be great guys, although not exactly the heroic types I had in mind for my television feature. Neither of them had had any previous experience at trapping elk, but, as the official who had hired them probably asked himself, who has? They were both college students, majoring in zoology, and had taken the elk-trapping job for the summer as a means of acquiring some experience in the field. Mostly what they had acquired was a deep and intense hatred for elk.

"We've seen all the elk we ever want to see," Mort told me.

"We've seen a whole lot more elk than that," Wally put in.

"I stand corrected," Mort said.

As we sat around the campfire that evening, Mort explained the trapping procedure to me. Basically, it consisted of luring an elk into a big corral with a salt bait rigged up in such a way that it dropped the corral gate behind the animal. The trappers would drive the elk into a confining chute, where a tag was attached to its ear and a bright orange collar fastened around its neck. Then it was released.

"I hate to say this, fellas," I said, "but it all sounds rather boring."

"Boring isn't the word for it," Wally said. "I've had more excitement planting potatoes!"

Egads, I thought. Here I had risked my life and practically destroyed my car in the hope of shooting some exciting footage of men and elk in hoof-to-hand combat, and now it turned out to be nothing more than a tedious routine! Even though I had been in the television business but a short while, I knew that, above all else, there were high standards of accuracy and truth and credibility to be maintained. One simply did not attempt to distort reality. So what that I had risked my life! So what that I had ruined my car! So what that I was about to lose my job! So what that we would have to fake it!

"How good are you fellows at feigning excitement?" I asked. "Let me see you do your bug-eyed-with-terror look."

I must say that I was rather surprised the next morning when, at the crack of dawn, Mort leaped from his sleeping bag and strode briskly out of the tent in the manner of a man eager to be about his business. Perhaps, I thought, these two elk trappers take their job more seriously than they let on. After all, their nearest boss was a good day of hard travel away. There was nothing to prevent them from sleeping in until ten or eleven if they wished.

Then Mort returned and climbed back into his sleeping bag.

"Get the fire going already?" I asked.

"What for?" Mort said. "We don't usually get up until ten or eleven. After all, our nearest boss is . . ."

"I know," I said.

Mort had exaggerated slightly. By ten, we were hoofing our way up a mountain so steep the trail was only eighteen inches away from my nose. At each gasp I stripped small pine trees bare of needles. I had charley horses that could have run in the Preakness. My tongue felt like a strip of smoked jerky. And most tiresome of all was that Mort and Wally strolled along, whistling and singing, and tossing a Frisbee back and forth.

We eventually arrived at the elk trap, which looked more like one of those stockades pioneers used for defense against the Indians. And it contained an elk! A huge cow was rushing back and forth, the whites of her eyes flashing with fear and rage.

"We caught one!" I shouted. "We caught an elk!"

Mort and Wally stared disgustedly, first at me and then at the elk.

"Listen, I don't want to disappoint you or anything," Wally said, "but this is going to be real boring. I wouldn't even bother setting up your camera if I were you."

He had disappointed me. "Well, since I've come this far I might as well shoot whatever I can."

While Mort and Wally ran around the trap, shouting and throwing small stones at the elk, trying to drive it into the confining chute at one end, I shot some rather dull film of the activity, then set my camera up next to the chute so I could get some good close-ups of the elk. Eventually, the cow, apparently thinking she saw an escape route, charged into the chute. Wally rammed a pole through the chute behind her to keep her from backing out and Mort slid another pole across the chute above her to keep her from jumping while the various paraphernalia were attached.

"Are you sure she can't get out of there?" I yelled at Mort, who was about to attach a bright orange collar to the elk.

"No way," Mort shouted back. "These poles are six inches thick. Take an elephant to break one of them. I told you this was going to be boring."

KerrAACK!

The elk had just snapped the pole that crossed the chute above her. Then, like a four-legged mountain climber, she went up the ten-foot-high wall of the chute, where she bashed another pole in two with her head, making an opening about the size of a basketball.

"She's getting out!" I yelled.

"No way," Mort said, calmly. "That hole is too small for her to get—"

Before he had finished the sentence, the elk had wriggled through the hole and was plummeting toward us! Even as the shadow of the descending elk expanded around us, I switched the camera to ON. This was my chance!

For ten seconds, chaos reigned. First, the elk was on Mort and Wally. Then Mort and Wally were on the elk and the elk was on me. Wally went by with the elk after him and Mort after the elk. I was going up a tree and the elk was coming down. There were shouts and bellows and grunts and groans; there were curses that must have stunted the growth of trees. Then the cow got her bearings and set a straight course for the Continental Divide, leaving me on my back in the dust, Wally perched on top of the elk trap, and Mort wearing the orange collar. And I had it all on film!

"Geez!" Hat said as we previewed my film back at the station. "What was that bit there?"

"That round thing that shot past? I think it was a close-up of a dust-coated eyeball. Now this blur here is where I jumped a log. That odd shape that flashed by was Mort with the elk on his shoulders! This is a great shot of some dust and blue sky. And here—"

I glanced at Hat, who was studying me thoughtfully, probably wondering how he could ever have so misjudged my talent as a television reporter.

"You know something?" he said.

"What's that?" I said.

"Five years isn't all that long. And besides, I could use the rest."

The Short
Happy Life of
Francis Cucumber

Almost every day the boy, Ace, would come over to the Jiffy Trading Post, and he and I would sit on the steps and talk. I remember one October morning in particular.

"What is it like to be a hunting guide?" Ace asked.

"It's very good to be a hunting guide," I said, "but the hard thing is to guide well and true and honorably."

"I wish you would stop talking like a Hemingway character," he said. "Nobody talks that way anymore."

"In the old days, everyone talked like a Hemingway character," I said.

"They don't anymore," Ace said.

"Yes," I said, "I know. It's sad."

"You're the only person left who still talks like a Hemingway character," he said. "You still talk that way. It makes me sick."

"I don't give a – – – –," I said. "I'll talk how I please."

"You don't have to use the dashes with me," he said. "I know that word."

"Do you know all the words?" I asked him.

"Yes," Ace said. "I know ———— and ———— and ———— and ——— and ————."

"That's very good," I said. "How about ——————————? Do you know that one?"

"I do now," he said. "That's a real dandy."

"Remember, you only use that word when you are being charged by a rhino and have missed with the second barrel of your .455 Rigby. It is a large-caliber word."

"I'll remember," Ace said. "Now, tell me again how it is to be a hunting guide."

I told him again how it was to be a hunting guide. Ace never tired of hearing about what it was like to be a hunting guide, possibly because he always fell asleep after the first five minutes.

In the old days, as I told Ace, the hunting-guide business was much more fun. When you met another hunting guide out in the bush and he wanted to know how you were getting along with your client, he would ask, "Are you still drinking his whiskey?" Now the question is, "Are you still drinking his mineral water?" Mineral water has taken a lot of the fun out of the hunting-guide business.

"How long has it been since you've had a client?" Ace asked.

"Eighty-two days," I said.

"That's a long time to go without a client," he said.

"Yes," I said. "My luck has been very bad. At least a dozen times now I have taken parties of five into the bush and come back with parties of only two or three. It may be an omen."

"It may be that you are a bad guide," Ace said.

I laughed and playfully snatched his motorcycle helmet and held it high overhead. He made some sounds of annoyance but finally managed to get the chin strap loose and dropped to the ground. He rubbed his neck.

"Why you old——!" he said. "Why did you do that?"

"I did it because you are a wise-elbow," I said. "You have always been a wise-elbow, ever since I have known you. That is why you are twenty-two years old and still in the fifth grade."

Ace pointed up the street. "Hey, would you look at that!" he said.

I turned cautiously, keeping one eye on him, because he likes to play tricks, sometimes hitting me on the ear with a big board when my back is turned. He was not tricking me this time.

A chauffeur-driven Rolls-Royce was coming down the street. It pulled up next to the Trading Post, and a middle-aged man and a much younger woman got out. I had great difficulty not staring at the see-through blouse; the skin-tight, shimmering, gold pants; the diamond necklace and earrings. The woman wore a simple print dress and no jewelry. She was blond and tan and slender with large blue eyes and a fine nose. She was very beautiful.

I can always tell Southern Californians when I see them. There is something different about them. I nudged Ace and whispered, "Check the license plate."

"Oklahoma," he said.

"Just as I figured," I said. "There is something different about Oklahomans."

There is something different about Texans too. I remember the Texan I guided up into the Hoodoo

Mountains. He had money written all over him. After that I could never stand to look at another tattoo. I sometimes wonder whether he ever found his way out of the mountains.

The man and woman started walking toward me and Ace. I pushed my hat back with my thumb, leaned against the porch post, stuck a wooden match in my mouth and chewed on it. Fortunately, I still have lightning reflexes and was able to smother the flames in my mustache before they took my eyebrows. Apparently, the man and woman had not seen lightning reflexes before.

"Are you all right?" the woman asked.

I squinted through the smoke of my smoldering lip stubble and grinned at her. "Mumpht bim scowp an maw mouph cot fahr, har, har," I said casually.

The man and woman glanced uneasily at each other.

"What can I do for you folks?"

"We're looking for Wilson, the hunting guide," the man said.

"At your service," I said.

"Oh?" the man said.

"Oh dear!" the woman said.

The man said his name was Francis Cucumber and the woman was his wife, Dill. He was after a trophy mountain goat. Friends had told him that Wilson was the best hunting guide in these parts. With all due modesty, I confirmed the truth of what his friends had told him.

"My services don't come cheap, though," I told Cucumber. "I get fifteen dollars a day plus expenses. Colorful expressions and ironic remarks are extra."

"We'll take the package." Cucumber said.

We made arrangements to pick up the Cucumbers at their hotel the following morning. I knew Ace would want to go along to help with the camp chores but was too proud to ask. Finally, when he couldn't stand it anymore, he blurted out, "C'mon, let me go!"

I chuckled good-naturedly and released him from the half nelson. "You remember to mind your manners around the clients," I told him. Since he had only two manners, I figured minding them was not too much to ask.

"One thing puzzles me," Ace said.

"What?" I said.

"How come you told them your name was Wilson?"

"Because Wilson already has more clients than he can handle."

That night I prepared for the safari into the mountains by rereading Hemingway's African short stories. If you are to guide well and true and honorably, it is very important to read Hem's African stories. Sometimes, if you have not read Hemingway in a long while, you cannot think of anything ironic to say to your clients. Clients become very upset with a guide who does not speak with irony, even when he doesn't get them lost in the mountains. Once, some clients and I were lost for three weeks and I ran out of ironic remarks and had to fall back on my knock-knock jokes. It is very dangerous to tell lost hunters knock-knock jokes, because sometimes they will charge you without warning and attempt to stuff used socks in your mouth. That is why you never go into the mountains without a good supply of ironic remarks.

The next morning we rode up into the Hoodoo Mountains and in the beginning everything went well and I thought we were going to have a fine hunt. Then Cucumber began to complain about his feet dragging on the ground.

"That is because your legs are long and the burro's are short," I explained.

"I know what the reason is," Cucumber snapped. "What I want to know is, why don't you let me ride the horse and you ride the burro?"

Clearly, the man was not without a sense of humor and I complimented him on his clever jest.

"It is a very good sign that you can make jokes even after the toes of your boots have worn off," I said. "You joke well."

"———————————!" Cucumber shouted.

I glanced swiftly around to see if we were being charged by a rhino, which is rare in Idaho. There was no sign of one. Already Cucumber was beginning to hallucinate. I had often observed this tendency in clients before, but never so early in the hunt.

That night we camped by a small mountain lake. While Ace and I prepared supper, Cucumber and Dill got into a furious argument. At one point I heard her scream, "How could you be such a fool as to get us into this mess! Anybody can see that that idiot doesn't know anything about guiding!"

That raised my dander. For one thing, this was only the fifth time I had brought Ace along on an expedition. You couldn't expect him to know anything about guiding with so little experience, even if he weren't an idiot. Ace didn't seem to mind what had been said about him, or so I judged from the fact that he burst into loud guffaws.

I fixed my famous Whatchamacallit stew for supper

and Cucumber and Dill even complained about that. Both of them said it upset their stomachs. If they had just tasted it, though, I'm sure they'd have found it not only hearty but delicious.

After supper we sat around the fire and talked and drank mineral water.

"Tomorrow we will be in goat country," I said. "The goats are very fine and white and beautiful this time of year and they are like patches of snow against the gray rock of the cliffs, and sometimes they are actually patches of snow, and then you know you are not yet in goat country at all, which is very discouraging after you have spent the day climbing a rock cliff."

"Huh?" Cucumber said.

"Egads!" Dill said.

"I have known hunters to shoot the patches of snow after they have climbed the cliffs," I said. "They do not laugh when they shoot the patches of snow either but are very serious about it and sometimes they even cry, which is bad for the morale of the other hunters."

"I'll bet," Dill said.

"The way you tell the goats from the patches of snow is that the patches of snow don't move or go 'baaa,' " I said.

"Go 'baaa'?" Cucumber said. "How far is it back to the road?"

"You don't understand," I said. "There are no goats between here and the road. Now, we'd better turn in. Tomorrow we must climb the cliffs and find the goats and we must hunt well and true and honorably."

"Your manner of speech reminds me of someone I've read somewhere," Dill said. "I think it's . . . it's . . ."

"Yes?" I said.

". . . Abigail Finley Dunlop!" she said.

"Well, enough of this silly prattle," I said sternly. "Let's hit the sack. We've got a gut-buster of a day ahead of us tomorrow."

"Ain'tcha gonna talk like a Hemingway character no more?" Ace asked. "I was startin' to like it."

"Shut up and douse the fire," I said ironically.

Shortly after sunup the next morning, Ace and I discovered that the Cucumbers had stolen my horse and vanished without a trace. Naturally, I was furious. What really made me mad, though, was not my clients' act of ingratitude and treachery and deceit but that my horse was the only one who knew the way home. Even worse, I couldn't get Ace to shut up: "It is not enough to guide well and true and honorably," he said. "You must also know which direction is the north and which direction is the south, and it is good, too, if you can tell east from west. Never ask for whom the bell tolls . . ."

The Arkansas Prank Hound

My cousin Buck was three years older than I. When we were growing up he was the smartest person I knew or ever expected to know. Buck was a walking university. There wasn't anything he didn't know or couldn't figure out. He was amazing. Of course, that was back before his mind started to go bad. His mind started to go bad about the time I entered high school and began to detect certain flaws in the information he dispensed to me. When I pointed these flaws out to him, he said even he had noticed some deterioration of his intellect.

As the years went by, Buck's IQ continued to plummet, eventually leveling out at what he termed average but what I would judge to be a whole lot closer to the intelligence of asparagus than of genius. But no matter. The portion of Buck's intellectual history that we are concerned with here is the early period, when he still knew everything.

In those early days I followed Buck around constantly, listening to him discourse on such matters as sex, life, death, hunting, fishing, sex, outer space, cars, sex, motion pictures, horses, dogs, motorcycles, and sex. Even though Buck knew everything about everything, he did seem to favor certain subjects. Wildlife, for example, was a specialty of his. One time we saw a funny-looking little mouse hopping along through the grass.

"What kind of mouse is that?" I asked Buck. "See the way it hops!"

"That's called a hop mouse," Buck said without even a moment's pause.

The speed with which Buck could identify even the rarest and most obscure of species was something to marvel at, but no more than his knowledge of wildlife physiology.

"How come that mouse hops instead of runs like a normal mouse?" I would ask.

Without a second's hesitation, Buck would explain, "'Cause it's got a different kind of hinges on its hind legs."

"Hinges?"

"Yeah, hinges. If you ain't about the most ignorant kid I ever knowed! Hinges is what lets legs bend."

Buck knew all about feeding habits, too.

"What do hop mice eat, Buck?" I asked.

"Just your regular mouse food—grass, roots, bread, cheese."

Buck's real area of expertise was dogs, hunting dogs in particular. What Buck didn't know about hunting dogs you could fit in the eye of a needle and still poke a camel through. His own hunting dog was a rare and expensive breed, the Arkansas Prank Hound. Buck always had to laugh about the way he fooled the man who sold him the dog. The man was sitting in an old pickup truck when Buck happened by and stopped to admire the pup.

"I bet you never seen a pup like this un," the man said.

"No, sir, I ain't," Buck admitted. "What kind is it?"

The man cast an appreciative eye down at the pup and after a thoughtful pause said, "Why, this is what you calls your Arkansas Prank Hound. Bet you ain't never even heard of the breed before."

"Course I have," Buck said, because he knew all the dog breeds there are. "Pretty good dogs, are they?"

The man's eyebrows shot up. "Good? Why, they is the best!"

"I mean are they good hunters?" Buck said.

"You wouldn't believe how good they are," the man said. "My goodness, the Arkansas Prank Hound does everything for the hunter but load his shotgun, and he'd do that too if you showed him how. But the main thing about the Prank Hound is it knows how to talk. You take most bird dogs, about all they can do is point the bird, right? But the Prank Hound, he'll come right out and tell you, 'There's two ringnecks and a hen hidin' in that tall grass over there.' Their one fault is sometimes they'll argue with you about who's gonna retrieve the bird, you or them. They ain't above makin' a nasty remark either when you miss an easy shot."

"You don't mean they talk real human talk, do you?" Buck said.

"Well, no, it's not exactly human talk. It's dog talk. The thing is, it don't take you no time at all to learn it."

"I don't suppose you'd consider selling the pup?"

"I surely do hate to," the man said. "But I've fallen on hard times lately. My house burned down and I lost my job and my heart has been actin' up on me. I suppose if somebody came along and offered me five hundred dollars for the pup I'd have to sell him."

"Gee," Buck said, "all I got is three dollars."

"That's close enough," the man said, thrusting the pup into Buck's hands. "Of course, I'd have to hold out for the five hundred if his papers hadn't burnt up in the fire."

Buck had to laugh as he told me later. Here he had foxed the man out of a five-hundred-dollar dog for three dollars, and all the time he had another two dollars in his pocket. Besides knowing everything back in those days, Buck was *shrewd!*

Buck named the pup Gooch. We could scarcely wait for the dog to grow up and start talking. Every other day or so, I'd go over to Buck's house and ask him, "Has Gooch said anything yet?"

Buck would look down at his dog. "Nothin' worth mentioning."

Now there are a great many cynics in the world who might assume that Gooch's previous owner had lied to Buck about the dog's ability to talk. After about a year in which Gooch had not uttered even the most casual of remarks, I was starting to become one of those cynics. One day I said to Buck, "I don't think Gooch is ever gonna talk! I think that man lied to you! He pulled a fast one on you, that's what he did."

Buck, of course, was unaccustomed to having me speak to him in that way. Being three years older than I, he had no trouble pointing out the flaws in my reasoning.

"This here is an Arkansas Prank Hound, ain't it?"

"Yes," I had to admit.

"And all Arkansas Prank Hounds know how to talk, don't they?"

"Yes," I had to admit.

"So it stands to reason that Gooch is gonna start one of these days, don't it?"

"Yes," I had to admit. Only one question remained in my mind. Would I have had to admit all those things if Buck hadn't been twisting my arm?

Shortly after that incident, however, it turned out that Buck had been right all along about Gooch. The dog did know how to talk! It was about the most remarkable thing I ever witnessed.

I had stopped by Buck's house in my usual fashion to ask him if Gooch had said anything yet.

"Why, yes, he did," Buck replied. "It wasn't nothin' important. Just your usual dog talk."

"He *talked*?" I shouted.

"Sure," Buck said. "Actually, he's been talking for several months now. It was just that I didn't understand Arkansas Prank Hound. I was expectin' him to say somethin' in American, until it suddenly occurred to me that he don't speak American. Then I got busy and started studying the sounds he was makin' and right away I figured out a few words. Now I can understand just about anything he says."

I looked at Gooch in amazement. "What does he talk about?"

"Oh, just the neighborhood dog gossip," Buck said. "It was kind of boring, to tell you the truth, particularly if you don't care any more than I do about what nasty things the Whites' dog wrote on their gatepost."

"Well," I said, "pheasant season's open. Let's take him out hunting and then he'll have something interesting to talk about."

Buck said that sounded like a pretty good idea. He went in the house and got his single-shot 16-gauge and we headed for the stubble fields south of town. Gooch walked along behind us, not saying anything. As we passed an alley, the dog spotted a cat and took off after it barking for all he was worth, a sum I still believed to be at least five hundred dollars.

"What's he saying?" I asked Buck, who was yelling at the dog to come back.

"Huh?" Buck said. "Oh, you're too young to hear language like that. I don't know where Gooch picked up some of them words. I just hope there ain't any ladies in this neighborhood who understand Prank Hound."

When Gooch finally caught up with us, we were already out to the stubble fields. He rushed up to Buck whining and yapping.

"I don't care what that cat called you," Buck told him. "I want you to tend to business. And furthermore, cut out using them swear words! Now get out there and do some hunting."

Gooch made a woofing sound.

"Oh, all right, *please* then!" Buck said.

It wasn't long before Gooch flushed a pheasant. I might have been mistaken but I thought the dog had stepped on the bird with his hind foot. In any case, Gooch jumped around yelping in fright and snapping his jaws in the empty air. He flushed another three pheasants in approximately this same manner, never once first saying a word to either Buck or me about a bird being anywhere in the area. As we were trudging back home without Buck having had a chance to fire a single shot, Gooch trotted happily along ahead of us, possibly singing a Prank Hound folk tune. If so, I couldn't make out either the tune or the words.

"I'd sure hate to sell ol' Gooch," Buck said, "but I could probably let you have him for five hundred dollars. Ain't every kid owns a talking dog."

"All I've got is a quarter," I said.

"That's close enough," Buck said.

"It's my lucky quarter and I can't give it up," I told him.

Actually, it wasn't my lucky quarter at all. I just couldn't take advantage of one of my very own relatives, particularly one whose mind was starting to go bad.

Well, Excuuuuse Me!

It has come to my attention that some of you anglers are forgetting your manners. You offenders know who you are, so I won't mention any names, but I want this crude behavior to stop immediately.

Perhaps it is time to review the basics of fishing etiquette, for the benefit of those of you who have forgotten them and for the youngsters just getting started in the sport.

Let us begin with a typical situation. Your fishing partner has laid claim to the only hole on the stream that seems to be producing any fish. He has pulled three nice rainbows from the hole and is walking around on his knees, either because he doesn't want to spook the remaining fish with the sight of his profile or because he is praying the fish will keep biting.

You haven't had so much as a strike all day, and you know your partner will be giving you nonstop lectures for the next month on how to improve your fishing

technique. What to do? Climbing up the cliff behind
your partner and throwing a large rock in the hole is
considered a breach of fishing etiquette. Furthermore,
it will be difficult to convince the offended party that
you threw the rock in the hole accidentally. The main
reason it will be difficult is that a person can't think
clearly while fleeing for his life.

According to proper fishing etiquette, you must
accept your partner's good luck gracefully. Call out to
him and offer encouragement and compliment him on
his technique. "WONDERFUL CAST THERE, BOB!"
you might yell. "I'LL BET YOU'RE GOING TO CATCH
A REAL MONSTER OUT OF THAT HOLE!"

Since he may not be up on his fishing etiquette,
Bob's response might be to grimace, shake his head furiously, and put his finger to his lips in the universal
gesture of asking for silence. Or he may use some other
universal gesture, depending upon his knowledge of
fishing etiquette. In any case, don't fall into a sulk, because that is the worst of bad sportsmanship. Merely
start crashing through the brush toward him, yelling,
"WHAT, BOB? WHAT DID YOU SAY? GO AHEAD
AND MAKE ANOTHER OF THOSE WONDERFUL
CASTS OF YOURS! I'LL BET THERE'S A FIVE-
POUNDER RIGHT OUT THERE WHERE THE TOP
OF MY SHADOW IS FALLING ON THE WATER!"

You may be surprised to learn that such gentle-
manly and polite conduct can be even more effective
than the loutish behavior of throwing a big rock in the
water.

Anglers often carry secrecy so far that it falls into
the realm of unsportsmanlike conduct. Some fishermen
I know laugh fiendishly and refuse to divulge the kind

of fly they have hit upon that happens to be producing fish at the moment. Such behavior is disgraceful. There is absolutely no reason to laugh fiendishly when a simple, inscrutable smile will do. In the rare instances when I'm the one with the right fly, I like to explain to the other anglers, as I land another trout, that much of the pleasure of fishing is to solve for one's self the mystery of what the fish are taking. It would subtract from their pleasure if I solved the mystery for them, I say, smiling inscrutably.

Of course, this patient explanation doesn't work on all anglers. Take Retch Sweeney, for example. His approach to solving the mystery is to say, "Yeah, right, sure," as he wrestles me to the ground, hauls in my line, and takes a look at the fly. Retch cares nothing for mystery and even less for fishing etiquette.

When asked what fly you are using, the polite thing to do is to open your fly book and hand a fly to the person making the request. He will be so pleased by your openness and generosity that he will respond in kind when the time comes for you to ask him what kind of fly he is using. As he hands you the fly, don't stare at it in astonishment and exclaim, "A turkey feather lashed to a Number two hook?" Otherwise, he will respond by saying, "Yes, it works just as well as the horsefeather fly you gave me. Maybe even better."

Here is another situation that often comes up. You have forgotten your lunch and are starving when you get back to the car first after a long day of fishing. Your partner's lunch is sitting there in plain sight on the front seat as a deliberate temptation to you. He could have followed his usual practice of hiding it under the spare tire of his car or in the engine compartment, where you always found it anyway. But leaving it on the front seat is practically an invitation.

You open the lunch sack tentatively and peer in. There are two sandwiches, a piece of cake, and an orange. The question is, should you eat one of the sandwiches? The piece of cake goes without saying, and the orange you will leave for him, but should you eat one of the sandwiches? The answer is to eat one. If you eat both sandwiches, you have violated fishing etiquette, and even worse, you may have to walk home.

Should you help ladies in and out of boats? The new social standards permit women to open their own doors, and it follows that they should be allowed to get out of boats unassisted. I, however, tend to be chivalrous by nature and always reach out a hand to steady the woman I fish with as she climbs from boat to dock. It makes her feel more secure and less likely to drop the rods and tackle boxes.

Suppose you do inadvertently commit a fishing faux pas. Many anglers are totally at a loss in such a situation and blunder about saying, "Gee, I'm sorry! How clumsy of me!" Such abject apologies only cause embarrassment in most fishing circles. It is far better to treat the mishap in a jovial manner. Here are a few apt responses for a variety of circumstances.

"Great leap, George! If I hadn't bumped you off the rock, I'd have never known what a fine athlete you are. Need a little more practice on the landings, though. Heh heh."

"Three-hundred-dollar rod, huh? Didn't feel like much more than a dollar ninety-eight when I stepped on the tip. Ho ho. Seriously, though, I've heard it improves the action of expensive rods if you break about three inches off the tip like I did there. Now, you just dry your eyes and see if that ol' rod doesn't actually cast better."

"Oh, I don't know, I think you look rather rakish with a bass plug in your ear."

"George, you won't believe what I did! Prepare yourself for a laugh. I forgot I had your square-stern canoe on top of the car, and I started to back into the garage. What? Yeah, I know it wasn't square-stern, but it is now! Get it, George?"

In all of these instances, you will note that the mishap is dealt with in a bluff and hearty manner, which your fishing companions will appreciate much more than they would humble apologies. If they don't happen to be familiar with fishing etiquette, however, no harm is done, at least none that a good chiropractor won't be able to work out for you in half a dozen visits.

The Mountain Car

Budge Honeylip, proprietor of Honeylip's Auto Salvage and Junk Co., sold us the mountain car himself. As we said afterward, Budge was a man you could trust.

Retch Sweeney and I had bicycled out to Honeylip's prepared to deal with his head salesman and tow-truck driver, Slick Beasly.

"Sure as shooting, ol' Slick will try to pass off one of those junkers Honeylip intends to sell for scrap iron," I told Retch.

"Yeah," he said. "You got to watch a man like Slick Beasly."

"Here's what we'll do," I said. "As soon as Slick starts giving us the hard sell on some wreck, we'll just laugh cynically and start to walk away. Let me hear you laugh cynically, Retch. Okay, that's not bad."

Retch and I had worked in the hayfields for nearly the whole month of June in order to earn enough money to buy ourselves a mountain car. Our transportation situation had become critical when both our respective sets of parents had simultaneously refused to allow us to drive the family autos anywhere except on paved roads. They had ranted some nonsense about mud and rocks and tree branches and fenders and oil pans as their excuse. The problem was that our county didn't have all that many paved roads, and what there were didn't go anyplace interesting, such as to decent hunting and fishing areas.

The crisis forced us to indenture ourselves to a series of farmers, every one of whom was possessed of a maniacal obsession for extracting from his hired hands their last ounce of energy. If we so much as stopped for a drink of water and a bit of conversation, the farmers would yell at us to stop goofing off because they didn't want their hay to get snowed on before Retch and I got it in, which was ridiculous, since it was still only June.

Our suffering and exhaustion were almost too much to bear. Retch and I each contracted a blister, in fact. When we showed our injuries to the farmer of the day, all he did was to laugh cruelly and say that it was so rare and strange for blisters to rise up for no known reason he had a mind to send it in to *Ripley's Believe It or Not*. Farmers were an insensitive bunch.

Having come by our money through such hard labor, Retch and I were not about to be snookered out of it by some high-pressure salesman like Slick Beasly. By the time we had bicycled out Cemetery Hill Road to Honeylip's Auto Salvage and Junk Co., we had our plans laid. The main idea was to slip into the salvage yard and check out the cars before Slick even knew we were in the vicinity. That way we would be able to arrive at our independent judgments, without being confused by a barrage of sales talk.

Everything went well until we started examining the first car, opening and closing its doors, looking under the hood, kicking the tires, gazing in wonder at the miraculously low mileage recorded on the speedometer.

"Afternoon, gentlemen," a voice behind us said. "Anything I can help you with?" It was Slick, calmly leaning against a rusty Packard, pretending to clean his fingernails with a penknife.

"Oh, we're just looking," I said shrewdly.

"Too bad," said Slick. "I happen to have a nifty little number here that runs like a dream."

He slid into the car, started it, and gunned the engine into a banging roar. It sounded good.

Slick shook his head as he turned the key off. "A rich banker in town is supposed to stop out any time now and buy this vehicle for his spoilt brat of a kid. Oh, how I do hate to see them rich kids get everything! Shucks, I'd sell this car right now for half price just to prevent that from happening."

"How much?" I asked.

"Hunnert," Slick said.

Retch and I laughed cynically and started to walk away.

Then Budge Honeylip popped out of his office in the company's quonset hut. "Dang it all to heck, Slick," he yelled. "I got a good mind to give you the boot, trying to foist a car like that off on these boys for a hunnert dollars."

"But, boss . . . !" blurted Slick.

"Don't but me," yelled Budge. "You git on over to the shop and change the oil in the tow truck. Won't be nobody around there you can cheat out of their hard-earned money!"

Slick hung his head and slunk off toward the quonset hut. I felt sorry for him, but he had it coming.

Budge put his arms around Retch and me. "Now you boys just tell ol' Budge the kind of vehicle you're looking for."

"A mountain car."

"You mean like for hunting and fishing?"

"Yeah, you know, the kinda car that will go just about anywhere."

"Oh, you don't want something fancy then, something with fenders and all what might get caught in the brush."

"Naw," Retch said. "It don't need fenders."

Budge said in that case he had just the car for us. A lot of his customers were picky, he said, and wanted fenders and all the trimmings on their cars, but he could see we were practical, down-to-earth, no-frills men. In addition to all his other qualities, Budge could judge character pretty well.

The car he showed us had a bit fewer frills than we had expected. No seats, for example. A missing door. A glassless rear window. A lidless trunk. And, of course, no front fenders. There were, we would discover, other missing frills, but their absence was not immediately observable.

Budge set an apple box inside the car for a seat, climbed in, and started the motor for us. It sounded like a washing machine tumbling down a flight of stairs. Smoke billowed out from every crack and seam.

Budge stuck his head out of the cloud of smoke. "Course it needs a tune-up—*cough, cough*—but you two look like you might be pretty handy with tools. Seeing as how that ornery Slick tried to—*cough, cough*—pull a fast one on you, I could probably let you have this—*choke*—prime mountain car for, oh . . . forty dollars?"

We stared at him in disbelief. Forty dollars! For this car? He had to be out of his mind!

Budge apparently was reading our thoughts because he started to say, "On the other hand, now that I think about it, maybe I could—"

"We'll take it!" Retch blurted out.

"Yeah," I added quickly. "You said forty dollars. You can't change your mind now."

We could tell from the look of astonishment on Budge's face that he hadn't run into a couple of sharpies like us in a long while. Obviously, when he realized what a mistake he'd made, he had thought about raising the price, maybe doubling it. He even as much as admitted his blunder after we had completed the transaction: "I'll tell you something, boys. It ain't every day I sell a car like this one for forty dollars."

Scarcely believing our good fortune, Retch and I loaded the bikes into the back of the car and were driving off, when we saw Slick standing in the door of the quonset hut. His mouth gaped as he stared first at us, then back at Budge, then at us again.

We decided to give our mountain car a quick road test on Cemetery Hill. The hill was by no means as rugged as the terrain our mountain car was intended for, but it was sufficiently steep and winding, as may be judged from the fact that the hill did not have a cemetery on it. The name had been invented by loggers who had to drive trucks down the steep, twisting grade.

Our mountain car growled up the hill without difficulty, delighting us with its performance. At the top, Retch, who was driving, plowed the front of the car up a steep bank in order to get it turned around.

"Wow! Look at that! This thing is just like a tank!" he exclaimed happily. "Now let's see how it does going downhill."

One of the frills missing from the car turned out to be the brakes.

Immediately, I saw why there was no door on the passenger's side. Some passenger had undoubtedly kicked it off in his haste to abandon the car on a downgrade. Only two factors prevented me from leaping out: (1) a fierce determination not to abandon my friend, and (2) total paralysis. Sitting on the seatless floor of the car, I could look down through gaping holes and see the earth rushing past a few inches away. Even worse, on one turn, I could see sky rushing past. Somehow Retch managed to get down the hill without flipping us over. After we had coasted to a stop, we sat silent for a long while, savoring the sensation of breathing. Presently, a farmer drove up in a truck. He squealed to a stop and rushed over.

"You boys all right?"

"Yup," Retch said.

"You're lucky to be alive from the looks of it," the farmer said. "Your car's totally demolished!"

Retch and I smiled feebly but appreciatively. It isn't everyone who can joke like that and still keep a straight face.

Retch and I drove the rest of the way to his place in low gear. The trip was without further incident, except that while we were waiting for a train to go by on a crossing, Sheriff McGrady's head poked through the smoke on my side.

"I should've known," he said, recognizing me and Retch. "What in tarnation have you two gone and done now?"

"Just driving our mountain car home," I said.

"Car?" the sheriff said. "There's a car here? Why, for goodness sakes, so there is. What kind of fuel does it burn, wet leaves? Now, I don't wish to seem unkind, lads, but if I catch you driving this vehicle on the public roads again, *I'll skin the both of ya!*"

Sheriff McGrady had no great appreciation of mountain cars.

Retch's father was sitting on the front porch in his undershirt drinking a can of beer when we pulled into the Sweeney driveway.

"Well, what d'ya think of our new mountain car, Popper?" Retch shouted. "We practically stole it from ol' Budge Honeylip for a lousy forty dollars!"

Mr. Sweeney stared impassively.

"Pat and me, we're gonna get out your tools and tear it all down and put it back together, Popper. Course we'll need the garage, but I figure you can park your car out in the alley for a couple of days."

Mr. Sweeney continued to stare impassively.

I began to suspect that he had suffered a stroke. Then, slowly, his lips began to move. "Someday somebody will invent a pill," he said.

Weird! Retch and I attributed this muttered nonsense to a slight stroke or maybe temporary senility.

We worked on the mountain car for a week, dismantling it piece by piece and arranging the parts in neat order on the floor of the garage, and down the driveway, and around the lawn. Mr. Sweeney would come home in the evenings, park his car in the alley, stare balefully at us and dispersed parts of the mountain car, then go into the house muttering to himself about the invention of pills. The man was not well.

My fellow mechanic and I were not feeling all that great either. Bit by bit our confidence in being able to reassemble the mountain car eroded. Panic started to set in. We began to quarrel.

"The long gizmo with the holes in it bolts onto that big thing over there," Retch would say.

"You're crazy!" I'd yell. "The flat thingamajig with the do-hickies on it goes there!"

Nevertheless, the car was reassembled in a single weekend. All the gizmos and thingamajigs and do-hickies were bolted into their proper places with swift efficiency, if not actual frenzy. The work, however, was accompanied by a steady stream of creative cursing that turned the air of the neighborhood blue for weeks afterward.

Occasionally, Retch's mother would come out to the garage and complain about the vile invectives rolling up from the bowels of the mountain car. "Hush!" she'd cry. "The neighbors will hear!"

"I don't give a *bleep* if they do hear," Mr. Sweeney would reply. "Now hand me that box wrench, Retch, and be quick about it!"

"Sure thing, Popper. But are you certain that whatchamacallit goes there?"

"Shut up!"

Mr. Sweeney did a wonderful job of putting the mountain car back together, and it was almost as good as before. He even repaired the brakes.

To show our gratitude, we offered to take Mr. Sweeney along on our first fishing trip in the mountain car. His only response to the invitation was a long, quavering laugh that reinforced our doubts about his emotional stability.

The mountain car provided us with enormous pleasure, hauling us to the very ends of wilderness roads and, often as not, back again. We even gave the car a name, Mrs. Peabody, in honor of our favorite high school English teacher. Apparently, this caused no end of rumors about the teacher. For example, one day Retch and I were tossing back a couple of malts in Toby's Soda Fountain and discussing our favorite topic, the mountain car.

"I think Mrs. Peabody's rear end is about to go out," I said. Toby froze in mid-wipe on a glass he was drying.

"What makes you think so?" Retch asked. Toby cocked his head in our direction.

"Well, she was making these strange rumbling sounds when I had her out in the mountains the other day."

"You had Mrs. Peabody out in the mountains," Toby asked. "What for?"

"The usual thing," I said. "Retch and me take her out two or three times a week. Sometimes we stay out for days."

"For days?" Toby said. "You and Retch with Mrs. Peabody?"

"Sure," I said. "It's more fun that way. Gosh, Toby, maybe you'd like to come along sometime, too. You'd be more than welcome."

"I don't think my wife would like me going out with Mrs. Peabody."

"Oh," Retch said, obviously miffed. "You think you're too good for Mrs. Peabody. Just because she's old and shabby and got a few too many miles on her, you don't want to be seen out with us."

"Goodness no," cried Toby nervously. "And she's certainly not all that old. Thirty-five, I'd guess."

"Thirty-two," Retch said, his temper cooling. "Sure, I'll admit Mrs. Peabody needs some work done on her. In fact, my pop says he's going to grind her valves first chance he gets."

Toby's glass shattered on the floor. "Your father is going to grind her valves? I thought he was a bricklayer."

"Yeah, he's a bricklayer, all right, but he's gotten so he enjoys tinkering with Mrs. Peabody out in our garage. It's sort of a hobby with him."

Mumbling incoherently, Toby walked off to find a broom. It was obvious he didn't know much about mountain cars, so we never mentioned Mrs. Peabody to him again.

Our adventures with Mrs. Peabody in the two years we owned her are too numerous to mention here, so I will recount only the last.

Retch and I were grouse hunting with Mrs. Peabody up on Big Sandy Mountain. As we were driving along, a big blue grouse appeared at the edge of the road up ahead. Retch eased Mrs. Peabody to a stop on a turnout, and we grabbed our .22s and slipped out of the car. The grouse, in the meantime, had flown up into a spruce tree. Stealthily, we walked up the road, trying to pick out the dark shape of the grouse among the boughs. I inched around the far side of the tree, my rifle at the ready, but I still couldn't see the grouse. Retch was still standing on the road, impatient as always.

"Fire," he said.

"I can't even see it," I whispered. "Why should I fire?"

"FIRE!" Retch shouted.

"Fire yourself, you idiot, if you can see the grouse," I shouted back at him.

"Forget the dang grouse," he yelled, taking off down the road. "Mrs. Peabody is on fire!"

Indeed she was. Although Mrs. Peabody had always smoked, now there were tongues of flame licking the hood. We were too late to save her.

The loss saddened us, of course, but there were others who looked upon it as a blessing. Among these was the Forest Service whose lookout towers half a dozen times a summer would report Mrs. Peabody as a fire out of control. My mother, who referred to the mountain car as "a death trap," was much relieved to hear of its end. Retch's father could scarcely contain his joy. Budge Honeylip saw it as an opportunity to sell us another fine car. But perhaps the most relieved and delighted person of all was our high school English teacher.

The Christmas Hatchet

The best evidence I've been able to come up with that the human race is increasing in intelligence is that parents no longer give their kids hatchets for Christmas.

When I was a boy the hatchet was a Christmas gift commonly bestowed upon male children. In an attempt to cover up their lapse of sanity, parents would tell their offspring, "Now don't chop anything."

By the time this warning was out of the parents' mouths, the kid would have already whacked two branches off the Christmas tree and be adding a second set of notches to one of his new Lincoln logs.

It was not that the kid harbored a gene compelling him to be destructive. The problem was with the hatchet, which had a will of its own. As soon as the kid activated it by grasping the handle, the hatchet took charge of his mental processes and pretty much ran the whole show from then on.

Shortly after Christmas the kid would be making frequent trips to the woodshed with his father, and not to chop wood either.

"The hatchet did it!" the kid would yell as he was being dragged toward the woodshed by his shirt collar. "I was just walking through the gate and my hatchet leaped out and chopped the post!"

Some kids were gullible enough to try the old George Washington cherry tree ploy. "I did it with my own little hatchet," they would confess.

"I know," their father would say. "Now haul your rear end out to the woodshed!"

The moral most of my friends and I drew from the cherry tree story wasn't that George Washington was so honest but that his father was a bit slow. This showed that even a kid with a dumb father could grow up to be President.

The average length of time a kid was allowed to remain in possession of his hatchet was forty-eight hours. By then the hatchet would have produced approximately sixty bushels of wood chips, eight hundred hack marks, and a bad case of hysteria for the kid's mother. The youngster would be unceremoniously stripped of his hatchet, even as its blade fell hungrily on a clothesline post or utility pole, and be told that he could have it back when he was "older," by which was meant age twenty-seven.

Kids now probably wouldn't understand the appeal hatchets held for youngsters of my generation. If a kid today received a hatchet for Christmas, he would ask, "Where do you put the batteries?" He would have no inkling of the romance of the hatchet and what it symbolized to boys of an earlier time, presumably all the way back to George Washington.

In the time and place of my childhood, woodcraft still loomed large in the scheme of a man's life. A man sawed and split firewood for the home, of course, but more important, he could take care of himself in the woods. He could build log cabins and lean-tos and foot-bridges, chop up a log to feed a campfire, fell poles to pitch a tent on or to hoist up a deer or to make a stretcher to haul out of the woods the person who wasn't that good with his ax.

One of the best things you could say about a man back then was that he was a good woodsman. Being a good woodsman seemed to erase a lot of other character flaws.

"Shorty may have some faults," one man might say, "but I'll tell you this—he's a good woodsman!"

"Yep," someone else would observe. "Shorty is a fine woodsman, all right. If he made it to the mountains, I reckon it'll take the posse a month to root him out."

The ax was the primary tool of the woodsman. If he wished, a woodsman could go off into the woods with an ax and provide heat and shelter for himself and live a life of freedom and independence and dignity and not be at anyone's beck and call or have to comb his hair or take baths. Not that I recall anyone ever fleeing to the woods, not even Shorty, who was nabbed sitting on a barstool at Beaky's Tavern, still a long way from the mountains. But it was the *idea!* If you were good with an ax and a gun, of course, and a knife, you could always fall back to the mountains. What it was all about, un-derneath, was the potential for freedom, not the jived-up freedom of patriotic speeches but real freedom, one-to-one-ratio freedom, where man plucks his living di-rectly from Nature. Of course, sometimes Nature plucks back, but that's not part of this dream, this vision, as symbolized by the Christmas hatchet.

I first realized I needed a hatchet when I was five years old and my mother read me stories about the pioneers chopping out little clearings in the great forests of the land. Ah, I thought, how satisfying it would be to chop out a clearing, to chop anything, for that matter. My campaign for a hatchet began immediately and achieved fruition on my eighth Christmas.

Although I wasn't allowed to touch any of the presents before Christmas Eve, I had spotted one package that bore the general shape of a hatchet. Still, I couldn't be sure, because my mother was a clever and deceptive woman, once wrapping a new pair of long johns to look like an electric train. Was she pulling a fast one on me this time or had she truly lost her senses and bought me a hatchet?

It turned out to be a hatchet, a little red job with a hefty handle and a cutting edge dull as a licorice stick. Even as I unwrapped it, I could feel all the thousands of little chops throbbing about inside, pleading to be turned loose on the world.

"Now don't chop anything," my mother said.

Within minutes, I had honed a razor edge onto the hatchet and was overcome with a terrible compulsion to chop. Forty-eight hours later, the hatchet was wrenched from my grasp and hidden away, presumably to be returned to me sometime after I had children of my own.

A few days after Christmas I learned that my friend Crazy Eddie Muldoon, who lived on the farm next to ours, had also received a Christmas hatchet.

"Where is it?" I asked. "Let's go chop something."

"Uh, I got it put away," Crazy Eddie said. "Let's use yours."

"Uh, I loaned mine to my cousin for a while," I replied. "He said, 'You don't have a hatchet I can borrow, do you?' and I said, 'Sure.' "

"Sure," said Crazy Eddie, who was only crazy part of the time.

As good luck would have it, an epidemic of permissiveness swept the county the following summer and both Eddie and I regained possession of our respective hatchets. There were still plenty of chops left in the hatchets and the two of us wandered off down to our woodlot in search of a suitable recipient.

A large tamarack soared up uselessly on the edge of the woodlot, and Crazy Eddie said maybe it would be a good idea if we built an empty space in the sky where it was standing. As it happened, I had long nourished a desire to yell "Timberrrrrr!" at the very moment I sent a mammoth of the forest crashing to the ground.

"Your folks can use it for firewood," Crazy Eddie said, in an attempt to explain his motive for felling the tamarack. But I knew he too yearned to hear the thunder of a great tree dashed to earth; he, as much as I, was into chopping for the pure aesthetics of the thing.

We spent all day chopping away at the tamarack, with Eddie on one side, me on the other, our hatchets sounding like slow but determined woodpeckers. At noon I went home for lunch.

"What are you boys up to?" my mother asked, with no great show of interest.

"Chopping down a big tree."

"That's nice," Mom said. "Don't fight."

After lunch, Crazy Eddie and I were back at the tree again, chipping out a huge U-shaped gouge all the way around its circumference. We were both exhausted, sweating, standing in chips up to our knees, but we could see now it was possible to accomplish the task we had set for ourselves. The tree began to moan and creak ominously as the hatchets bit into its heartwood. By late afternoon the huge tamarack stood precariously balanced on a gnawed core of wood slightly thicker than a hatchet handle.

Neither Crazy Eddie nor I had the slightest clue as to the direction in which the tree might fall, which heightened our anticipation with the added element of suspense. We took turns charging up to the tree, whacking out a quick chip, and then dashing back to relative safety.

Suddenly we heard it: the faint, soft sigh that signaled the tree's unconditional surrender to our Christmas hatchets. A silence fell upon the land. High above us the boughs of the tamarack rustled. Crazy Eddie and I shivered happily. We had accomplished something momentous!

Crrrrrraaa . . . went the tree, beginning a slow tilt. We were now able to determine the direction of its fall, which wasn't particularly good. Eddie's father, a short while before, had built a fence between our woodlot and theirs and now, even though I had not yet studied plane geometry, I was able to calculate with considerable accuracy that the tree would neatly intersect the fence at right angles.

"You better yell 'timber,' " Crazy Eddie said, his voice trembling.

"Timmmm . . . ," I started to cry. Then we heard another cry. It was that of Eddie's father, who had come down to the woodlot to call him to supper.

"Eddieeeee!" his father called. "Crazy Eddieee! It's time for supperrrrr!"

Cr-r-r-r-a-a-a-a-A-A-A-A-ACK! went the tree.

"Eddieee!" went Eddie's father. "EddieeEEEEEE!"

The monstrous tamarack smote the earth with a thunderous roar, rising above which was the twanging hum of barbwire. Fence posts shot into the air fifty yards away. Eddie's father shot into the air fifty feet away.

"Bleeping bleep of a bleep!" screamed Eddie's father, introducing me to that quaint expression for the first time.

There is an old saying that cutting firewood warms you twice: once when you chop it and once when you burn it. Well, chopping down that tamarack warmed Eddie and me *three* times, and one of those warmings was a good deal hotter than when the wood burned.

I learned a good many things from felling that tamarack with my Christmas hatchet, perhaps the most interesting of which is that a barbwire fence is regarded by its builder as merely a barbwire fence until a tree falls on it. Afterward it is looked back upon as a priceless work of art, surpassed in beauty and grandeur only by the Taj Mahal.

My Christmas hatchet disappeared immediately after the great tree-felling but surfaced again a few years later when I was old enough to conduct my own camping trips. Much to my surprise, I discovered the hatchet was almost useless for cutting wood. It was as if Excalibur had been reduced to a putty knife.

The very next Christmas, I gave my little cousin Delbert the hatchet as a present.

"Wow!" he said. "A real hatchet of my own! Thanks a lot!"

"You're welcome!" I shouted after him as he raced away, homing in on a stand of shrubs in his backyard. "But don't chop anything!"

The Night Grandma
Shot Shorty

When I was a boy, we kept a loaded pistol in the house with which to dispatch criminals who might come prowling around late at night. We never killed any criminals with the pistol, but there was one near-fatality. Unfortunately, the victim was not a criminal, at least so far as we knew.

The caliber of the pistol was very large, at least .45—maybe .50—and magnum to boot. The pistol could put a hole in you the size of a grapefruit, if you were a criminal trying to force your way into our house late at night. At least that's what I told the guys at school. What I didn't tell them was that the gun was a figment of my mother's imagination.

My father had died when I was six, leaving me the lone male in a family of women—my mother and grandmother and a sister, who was six years older than I. If I have never become too excited over women's liberation, it is because I grew up surrounded by liberated females, all tough, hard, and fearless. Any one of them could have taught a graduate course in assertiveness training. My sister held a black belt in aggravation.

Our farm was situated about a mile from a railroad, and it was not unusual for tramps to stop by and ask if they could chop some wood in exchange for a meal. My mother, bless her heart, never once turned away a tramp unfed, but boy did those suckers chop wood! There were no free handouts at the McManus farm.

Even with all the tramps drifting into our place (staggering away three hours later with a baloney sandwich clutched limply in hand), Mom never saw any need for a gun as a means of self-protection. After all, she viewed the tramps as harmless, easy-going fellows, who, if spoken to with a proper measure of firmness, were capable of chopping a good deal of wood.

Then one day Mom went into town and hired three local criminals to build an extension onto the chicken house. When they were about half done with the project, she saw they had no skill as carpenters, paid them off, and sent them packing.

"We'll get you for this!" one of the criminals, a mean little man called Shorty, yelled back over his shoulder.

"Ha!" Mom responded.

The threat, however, caused some concern among the rest of the family. What would we do if Shorty came sneaking back in the middle of the night, intent on murdering us all?

"Oh, all right!" Mom said. "Here's what we'll do." She explained that if we heard any strange noises outside at night or someone banged on the door, my sister would sing out loud and clear, "Do you want the gun, Ma? Do you want the gun?" To which my mother would loudly reply, "Oh, you'd better give it to me! But be careful—it's loaded!"

This system worked rather well. Not only did the imaginary pistol frighten off any criminals making strange noises outside our house, but it gave several innocent late-night visitors a bad case of the shakes.

In fact, the imaginary pistol turned out to be more deadly than any of us expected. One night my mother was sitting up alone playing a game of solitaire, when suddenly there was a banging on the door. Mom, who never thought the imaginary pistol was necessary in the first place, got up and answered the door without bothering to wait for my sister to sound the alarm.

The visitor turned out to be a diminutive young fellow by the name of Little Ernie and he had a terrible tale of woe to tell. He had joined the Civilian Conservation Corps that summer and had been working with a CCC crew back in the mountains eradicating blister rust. Somehow, Little Ernie had managed to antagonize the rest of the crew, and they had taken him down and shaved off all his curly blond hair. He had left the camp in a huff, his cowboy hat wobbling loosely atop his ears.

As he recited the story to Mom, his voice rose and fell, quavering with rage. He also refused to remove his hat to allow Mom to survey the damage. In that time and place, it was considered the ultimate rudeness for a man to wear his hat in the house. This was to be a contributing factor in the misunderstanding shortly to follow.

After one last outburst of rage, Little Ernie pounded the table with his fist. Mom was getting tired of hearing about the atrocity and she told Ernie he could spend the night in a spare upstairs bedroom. She then went off to bed herself, neglecting in all the excitement to mention to Ernie that another upstairs bedroom was occupied by my Aunt Gladys, who was visiting, and Gram.

When the banging on the front door had first sounded, Aunt Gladys and Gram had sat "bolt-upright" in bed. Soon they heard a loud male voice full of rage and incoherence.

"It's *Shorty!*" Gram hissed to Aunt Gladys, who had been told about the threat. Aunt Gladys went pale and her hair tightened in its curlers.

"We'd better go help Mabel," she whispered.

They listened a bit longer to the mad ravings rising from the living room. Then they heard the dull sounds of blows being delivered.

"My God, he's killed her!" Gram gasped.

After a period of silence broken only by the tinny rattle of hair curlers, they heard booted feet begin to ascend the stairs.

"Oh!" Aunt Gladys whispered. "Now he's coming for *us!*"

Through the open door of their bedroom, Gram and Aunt Gladys had an unobstructed view of the stairwell. *Thump . . . thump . . . thump . . .* came the booted steps. Given their emotional state, it was perhaps understandable that Gram and Aunt Gladys would mistake the slow plodding on the steps to be a result of stealth rather than weariness and nervous exhaustion.

Slowly, the crown of a cowboy hat rose above the edge of the stairwell, a sure sign the intruder was a killer. No one else would wear a hat in the house. Then the head and shoulders came into view. There was only one thing to do.

Gram drew the imaginary pistol.

Employing the tone of voice she reserved for breaking up dog fights and ordering the family hog out of her flower gardens, she let Little Ernie have it.

"Hold it right there, Shorty," she snarled, "or I'll blow your head off!"

Three days later, Little Ernie had recovered enough to be ready and willing to go back to the CCC camp. By then, if he held a cup in both hands, he could get it to his lips without sloshing coffee all over himself. Much of his color had returned too. Since the stubble of his hair had leaped up half an inch when he heard Gram's command, he now looked as if he had a crew cut, although it was somewhat lighter in shade than his original blond curls. We never saw Little Ernie again, so I don't know if he ever fully recovered. Perhaps he was still peeved at Gram, thinking that by calling him "Shorty" she had been referring to his modest stature.

Mom got rid of the pistol soon afterward. She said it was too dangerous to have lying around the house, where a young boy or an old lady might get hold of it and accidentally kill somebody.

The Kindest
Cut of All

Hal Figby, a newcomer to our little gather-
ings down at Kelly's Bar & Grill, doesn't care
much for hunting or fishing. We don't hold that against
him, of course, and even go out of our way to treat him
just as if he were normal. He is soft-spoken, polite, does
everything in moderation, and in general seems to be a
perfect gentleman. Otherwise, he is a pretty decent sort
of guy. He's even good for a laugh occasionally, such as
the time we invited him down to Kelly's to watch the
Saturday night fights. He said later he had thought we
meant the fights would be on television! Broke us up.
That's just the sort of person Figby is. Still, we couldn't
have been more surprised when he committed the breach
of etiquette.

Half a dozen of us had stopped by Kelly's after a
hard day of fishing and were getting tuned up to spend
the rest of the evening testing out some new lies on each
other and maybe stretching a truth or two. Then Figby

showed up. Scarcely had he sat down than he began staring across the table at Retch Sweeney.

"Something wrong, Figby?" Retch asked, in a tone that killed somebody's promising lie in midsentence.

"Uh," Figby said, "it's just that nasty scar on your face. I was wondering how you got it."

We were dumfounded. Of all the stupid things we might have expected Figby to say, this was absolutely the worst. Here we had just got a nice start on a pleasantly sociable evening, and Figby had to blurt out something like that. Even Figby should have known you never ask a man how he got a scar on his face. A couple of the guys got up in disgust and walked out right then. I later regretted I hadn't gone with them, because I didn't have much stomach for what happened next. And I must say, Retch was unmerciful. He talked steadily about that scar for upwards of two hours. It was dreadful.

There is nothing a man, particularly an outdoorsman, enjoys talking about more than his scars. Every scar has a story behind it. I have heard some scar stories approximately the length of Churchill's *A History of the English-Speaking Peoples,* but such brevity is rare. Once a question has been put to an outdoorsman about one of his scars, the man will go on a binge of scar stories. He cannot tell about one scar and let it go at that. As soon as he has exhausted all the scars on his face, he will move on to the scars on his hands and arms, and once he has recited the history of each of them, he descends to his lower extremities, finally rolling up his pant legs to search for old scars he might have forgotten about.

It is for that reason that no outdoorsman will ever ask another about a scar.

There are certain constants in the telling of any

scar story. One is that the recipient of the near-mortal wound from which the scar was derived never uttered a sound during the ordeal: "So, there I was, my arm laid open elbow to wrist, and me not making a sound. Several of the younger fellows fainted dead away at the sight of it, and I couldn't help but smile. Then ol' Pap Wiggens got out a saddle-stitching awl and sewed up my arm with a length of catgut leader, and I didn't so much as say 'ouch.'"

It may be nothing more than a coincidence, but I have yet to hear a scar story in which the injured party admitted to bellowing like a bull moose with bursitis.

Another characteristic of the scar story is that the scar always is much smaller than the original wound. In fact, each time the story is told, the difference between the size of the scar and the size of the wound becomes increasingly greater, until you begin to worry that if the story is told one more time the original injury might prove fatal. I've seen outdoorsmen express real astonishment that they somehow managed to survive a wound that left a quarter-inch scar on an index finger. Once during a physical examination, I asked the doctor the cause of this phenomenon, and he spent the rest of the afternoon telling me about a tiny scar on his elbow left over from the time he nearly severed his arm. I hadn't realized until then that he was an outdoorsman. Afterward he gave me a prescription for some drops to clear up my glazed eyes.

Another feature of the scar story is that the teller always remembers to make a dry, humorous comment to his companions as they gape in horror at his damaged hide. "It's just a scratch" seems to be the standard dry, humorous comment. Obviously, you can't expect great creativity from an injured person.

One interesting and amusing characteristic of the scar story is how easily an outdoorsman can be reminded of one.

"Have you seen John's boat?" someone might ask.

"No," replies the outdoorsman, "but that reminds me. I don't believe I've ever told you how I got this scar on my cheek."

Persons unknowledgeable about outdoorsmen might assume that a boat played at least some slight part in the acquisition of the scar. When the story is at last over, they will ask, "But what about the boat?"

"What boat?" replies the outdoorsman. "Say, that reminds me of the scar on my ankle."

Speaking of boats, there's quite a story behind this scar on my thumb.

The scar is merely a small, whitish crescent just behind the knuckle. I must explain, however, that the scar remained the same size but my thumb grew. When it received the original wound, my thumb was only seven years old. To fully appreciate the gash on my thumb, you must visualize the scar superimposed on a little seven-year-old thumb. Then you realize how truly ghastly the injury was.

The scar happened like this. Crazy Eddie and I were planning our first camping trip. We had both been sentenced to second grade and were due to start serving our time the following week. When you're seven years old, second grade lasts for life and a day. (When I was eight, second grade lasted only twenty years, which was a great improvement.) We wanted to have one last fling before the doors shut behind us, and a camping trip seemed like a good idea.

Finding enough grub for the camping trip was the big problem. We dug a few potatoes out of the garden, and Crazy Eddie sneaked half a loaf of bread from his house. But we needed some meat. Fortunately, Eddie's father had hauled a dead horse into their barnyard a few weeks before. He had cut up most of the carcass to feed to the foxes he raised for furs, but there were still some good parts left. Eddie borrowed his father's hunting knife while his parents were away, and we went out to the barnyard to cut off a few steaks to roast on willows over the fire we hoped to build by rubbing two sticks together because we weren't allowed to play with matches. Eddie sliced off a nice round steak for himself without incident or accident. Probably one reason he didn't cut himself was that he used one hand to cut with and the other to hold his nose. The hand that holds the knife doesn't usually get cut, so the trick is to keep the other hand out of the way and occupied with some useful task like holding your nose. Foolishly, I tried to brush the flies off the steak I was cutting. The knife slipped and laid open my thumb to the bone.

I didn't cry. That was the first time I had been hurt that badly and didn't cry. I remember thinking, "Odd, I just cut my finger to the bone and I'm not crying."

Eddie wasn't very supportive in that regard. "Geez," he said, "all your blood is leaking out!"

That made me want to cry, but I didn't. Maybe I somehow knew that years later I would have this wonderful scar and I wouldn't want to remember that I cried when I got it.

"Don't it hurt?" Crazy Eddie asked, apparently because he couldn't deal with the fact that I wasn't crying.

I decided to compound his amazement by making a dry, humorous comment about the cut, but I couldn't think of any. "Naw," I said finally, "it's just a scra . . . a scra . . . I got to go home." And I went.

Two weeks later I finally thought of a dry, humorous comment, but by then we were in second grade and Crazy Eddie was too miserable to appreciate it.

During the years of my childhood, I picked up dozens of tiny scars, but none worth showing to anybody. All my friends were constantly getting neat scars. One time Crazy Eddie and I were floating a log raft down the creek. Suddenly, up ahead, we saw a strand of barbwire stretched across the creek about six inches above the water. Crazy Eddie, who was on the front of the raft, lay down and pressed himself against the logs so that he would pass under the wire. He didn't press hard enough. The barbs raked him fore and aft, particularly his aft. (He wasn't known as "Crazy Eddie" for nothing.) When I came to the wire, I calmly stepped over it, averting my gaze from the bits of Eddie left on the barbs. Eddie picked up an interesting set of scars from the experience, and he liked to claim later that he never uttered a sound during the ordeal. Maybe so, but the workers at a nearby sawmill went home early that day because they thought they heard the shriek of the quitting whistle.

Crazy Eddie continued to add to his collection of scars with knives, hatchets, saws, arrows, fishhooks, tree branches, sharp rocks, just about anything that had any potential at all for lacerating his skin. By the time we were in sixth grade, Eddie looked like a walking display of hieroglyphics. He was the envy of every boy in school.

I, on the other hand, had only one good scar, the one on my thumb. The problem with a scar on a thumb is that it is not easily called attention to. Once I was lucky enough to fall facedown in a pile of rocks and get a deep gash on my chin. I had high hopes for that wound, but bit by bit the scar faded and within six months had vanished.

"Thank heavens," my mother said. "I thought you might be disfigured for life." Mothers just don't understand about scars.

I have an excellent scar on one of my feet, a gift from a double-bitted ax. But a foot is one of the worst places to have a scar. How do you explain taking off your shoe and sock and placing a smelly foot up on a table so the scar can be noticed? I have often been asked for such an explanation and, failing to come up with one, have on several occasions been forcibly ejected from Kelly's Bar & Grill. A scar on your foot is more of a nuisance than anything. It is, as Shakespeare put it, the unkindest cut of all.

One of life's worst misfortunes is to get a truly fabulous scar in a place where no one except maybe your spouse can notice it, and spouses, like mothers, are generally unappreciative of scars. A classic instance of such a scar occurred when my friends Retch and Birdy and I were about seventeen. We had been fishing in a place that required that we drive through a series of hayfields, opening and shutting half a dozen gates along the way. Retch was driving his old 1933 sedan, and, because he was furnishing the transportation, he insisted that Birdy and I open and shut the gates. Birdy complained that this was an unfair labor practice and violated constitutional rights as they apply to hayfield gates. A heated argument ensued, and certain vile names were exchanged. When we arrived at one of the gates, Birdy got out, swearing that this was absolutely the last gate he was going to open and close.

"Ha!" Retch said. "We'll see about that. Lock all the doors so he can't get back in. We'll make him walk all the way to the next gate and we won't let him back in the car until he opens and closes it. *Heh heh!"*

With that, he started driving slowly across the hay-field toward the next gate. What happened next came as quite a surprise to Retch and me, since neither of us had ever guessed that Birdy might possess ambitions to become a stuntman.

Once he perceived what we were up to, Birdy raced after the bouncing sedan, making no attempt to conceal his fury. He climbed on the back bumper, worked his way up over the trunk, across the roof of the car, and down onto the hood. Once he was on the hood, he sprawled across the windshield to block Retch's vision.

His plot foiled and his vision blocked, Retch became furious. "Well, I'll fix him!" he snarled, pressing down on the gas pedal until we were bouncing along at nearly twenty miles an hour. Birdy reacted by turning his back to us and, now astraddle the hood, grabbed hold of the rain gutters on each side of the windshield to steady himself. Retch hit the brakes.

Birdy shot off the front of the hood as if from a catapult. He made a nice eight-point landing, counting two points for each bounce. Retch and I expected that he would rest there on the ground for a spell and contemplate the error of his ways. Instead, he instantly leaped up and launched into a wild and wonderful dance to the accompaniment of his own whoops and hollers.

That was when we remembered the hood ornament, one of those little jobs with the wings raised in simulation of flight.

The little wings gave Birdy a spectacular matched set of scars. Unfortunately, they were in a place where they were not likely to be noticed in the typical social situation. In the thirty years since, Birdy has not once had occasion to tell the story behind those scars. It seems like such a waste.

Scars are often interpreted as evidence that a man has lived dangerously. I totally dismiss my wife's assertion that they are more likely proof that he has lived dumbly. She knows nothing about the masculine mystique.

My hope is that the cosmetic industry will soon come up with false scars for men, much as it did with false beauty marks for women. It would be only fair, not to mention a lot less painful. But it probably wouldn't work. After all, who would want to tell about getting a scar from the Avon lady?

The Bush Pilots

Mostly what I wanted to be when I grew up was a mountain man, but there was one brief period, during the summer of my eighth year, when I gave serious consideration to becoming a bush pilot.

It was Crazy Eddie who got me to thinking about the bush-pilot business. He came up with the idea immediately after our ill-fated venture into deep-sea diving, which, among other consequences, produced a rare form of hysteria in the Fergusons' herd of milk cows: not only couldn't they be made to drink; they refused even to be driven to water. A veterinarian was brought in to offer an opinion, but, because he had no experience with the effects of deep-sea diving on cows, he failed to come up with a diagnosis. Had the vet thought to ask Crazy Eddie and me, as people usually did when inexplicable phenomena occurred within the range of our travels, we could have told him what was wrong with the Ferguson cows. They had the bends.

Since the reader may have some difficulty grasping the deeper psychological implications of my bush-pilot phase, an examination of the deep-sea-diving venture may provide some insights, particularly in light of the fact that both experiences involved traumatized cows.

In my own defense, I must report that the entire deep-sea-diving experiment was Eddie's idea. I was recruited at the last minute, to help with the testing, after Eddie had designed and assembled the diving outfit himself. Although the technology of the outfit would be too difficult for the lay person to understand, I will mention that its component parts consisted of an old milk pail, a tire pump, a length of garden hose, and two bags of rocks. Eddie said he needed me to work the tire pump while he descended into the depths of Sand Creek, the test site being a deep hole in the creek behind the Ferguson place. The hole was next to the bank on one side of the creek. The creek bottom tapered up from there onto a gravel bar on the opposite side, where the Ferguson cows came to drink. Through oversight, Crazy Eddie hadn't factored the cows into the experiment.

As Eddie and I stood on the bank staring down into the swirling dark waters of the hole, my friend could scarcely contain his enthusiasm.

"Boy," he said, "I can't wait to get down there and start exploring. This hole is a perfect place for pirates to hide a chest of treasure. Probably some pearls down there too, and gold and—"

"C'mon, Eddie, let me go first!" I blurted.

"Okay."

While he was helping me on with the milk-pail helmet, Eddie said he was letting me go first only because I was his best friend and that he wouldn't even consider doing such a favor for anyone else. I said I appreciated it and, sliding down over the bank, asked Eddie if he was sure the diving outfit would work.

"Yeah," Eddie yelled, starting to work the pump furiously. "But if it doesn't, can I have your bike?"

Still contemplating Eddie's little joke, I plunged into the hole. I sank swiftly into the cool, swirling darkness, the bags of rocks tied to my belt working wonderfully well. There were, however, some bugs in the rest of the outfit. The helmet offered limited visibility, since the only way to see out of it was straight down. Mostly what I could see was the level of water rising in the inverted milk pail, despite the *hiss hiss* of the air hose. Of even more interest to me at the moment was the distinct tactile impression of long, slimy tentacles of octopus slithering around my body. Thus distracted, and with the water in the helmet now lapping about my eyes, I scarcely touched bottom before setting a course toward the incline of the gravel bank on the far side of the creek. Even though I maintained the calm demeanor I thought appropriate to a deep-sea diver, the vigor of my movements caused silt and gravel to boil up in such a fashion as to effect major changes in the creek channel, or so Eddie later remarked.

It so happened that at that very moment, the herd of Ferguson cows was moseying down to the creek for a drink, apparently mildly interested in the frantic activities of the boy on the far bank but with no expectation of a streaming, slime-covered creature with an inverted milk pail on its head to be emerging from their watering place. As Crazy Eddie later related the spectacle to me, for I was too preoccupied with gasping to notice such things, the entire herd rose straight up eight feet in the

air, reversed direction, and to the accompaniment of a
cowbell rendition of "The William Tell Overture," disappeared over a distant hill. Oddly, the route of the
cows' departure was marked in later years by an unusually lush growth of grass. The wondrous vitality of
the swath of grass became something of a local mystery,
as did the refusal of the cows to go anywhere near the
creek for two weeks afterward, despite the maniacal ex-
hortations on the part of Mr. Ferguson to get them to
do so and save him the chore of carrying water to them.

Naturally, Crazy Eddie was disappointed in the performance of his diving outfit.

"Maybe it was my fault," I said, untying the bags
of rocks from my belt. "I probably did it wrong. Why
don't you give it a try and let me stand on the bank and
pump air?"

Eddie thought for a moment. "Gee, I would," he
said, "but it's, ah, getting on toward suppertime. Besides,
I've been thinking that maybe I'd rather be a bush pilot
than a deep-sea diver."

As we walked home, dragging the deep-sea-diving
outfit behind us, Crazy Eddie suggested that maybe I
would want to go into the bush-pilot business with him.
He explained how it would work. "We'll have this plane,
see, and we'll fly hunters and fishermen back into the
wilderness. We'll land on gravel bars in rivers and in
little clearings in the forest, and the hunters and fishermen will be scared to death, but afterward they'll say,
'Boy, you sure know how to handle this plane!' and we'll
just laugh like it was nothing. But we won't work all the
time. Whenever we want, we'll go fishing and hunting
ourselves. It'll be great!"

Already I could feel myself getting caught up in

Eddie's dream. "But where will we get the plane?" I asked. "We don't have any money."

"We'll have to build it. Of course, we'll start off with just a little plane, one we can use to practice our flying with and landing on gravel bars and small clearings in the forest. That can be tricky. Come on over to my place tomorrow and we'll start building the plane."

"Sounds good to me," I said, tilting my head to one side and batting some creek water out of my ear.

I did have some doubt that Crazy Eddie and I could actually build an airplane. As it turned out, though, Eddie was an aeronautical genius. When I showed up the next morning, he had already drawn up the plans on a sheet of Big Ben tablet paper. He said he had based the design on a plane in a comic book story about a bush pilot. It looked swell.

"Where will we get the motor?" I asked.

"My dad's got an old washing-machine motor out in his shop," he replied. "We can use that, and whittle a propeller out of a board." That sounded reasonable enough. I felt guilty about having doubted Eddie's engineering skills.

"We'll start off with a glider, though," Eddie continued. "After we've practiced landing the glider a few times, we can hook up the washing-machine motor to it, and work on our takeoffs."

"But we'll need some high place to launch the glider from," I said. "What can we use?"

"No problem," said Eddie. He pointed to the roof of the towering Muldoon barn. Why hadn't I thought of that? I supposed it was because I wasn't an aeronautical genius.

The finished plane bore only a slight resemblance

to Eddie's design, possibly because our escalating anticipation of the forthcoming flight caused us to rush construction. Then again, it may have been the limited supply
of materials available to us: two apple crates for the
cockpits, an empty dynamite box for the motor housing,
two long pieces of shiplap siding for the wings, a short
board on a rusty hinge for the tail, and the rear wheels
and axle from Eddie's wagon for the landing gear. All
things considered, the bush plane looked exceptionally
airworthy.

It had soon become obvious to us that the completed plane would be too heavy for the two of us to
carry up to the ridge of the barn roof, so we assembled
the parts up there. The roof had two angles to it, one
about 30 degrees, and the other, the lower one, a steep
45 degrees or so. A shed roof was attached to the bottom
edge of the barn roof. Near the eave of the shed roof,
Eddie and I built a ramp that, once our plane had picked
up sufficient speed in its descent, would loft us up into
the clouds, where we would spend the rest of the day
riding the wind. Toward evening we would find a gravel
bar or a small clearing in the woods on which to practice
our bush-pilot landing.

With the aid of a ladder, we managed to get all the
parts of the plane up to the ridge of the barn roof and
assembled. The bush plane, pointed nose-down, was held
in place by means of a rope attached to a weather vane,
the knot in the rope being tied in such a manner that
the pilot needed only to jerk an end of the rope to release
the craft for its descent.

The activities on the roof of the barn provoked
much interest among the resident population of spar-
rows, who kept darting about and offering advice and

encouragement, but because the construction had taken place on the side of the barn away from Crazy Eddie's house, his parents, both of whom seemed to suffer from severe nervous disorders, knew nothing of our activities.

Late in the afternoon, the plane, straining at its tether, was finished. Crazy Eddie, crouched beside me on the slope of the barn roof, could scarcely contain his excitement over the first flight.

"Boy, it'll be great," he said. "Just think about it. Soaring around up there in the clouds, looking down at the patchwork of fields, all the cars and animals and stuff real tiny like, and—"

"Yeah," I said. "You'll have to tell me all about it after you land."

Crazy Eddie looked at me. "The wind blowing in your hair, the plane sailing along like a hawk."

"Hmmm," I said. "Maybe we both should go. The plane's got two cockpits, after all."

"Well, okay," Crazy Eddie said, with what I took to be a slight ebbing of enthusiasm.

"Say, maybe your folks would like to see us test the plane," I suggested. "Why don't you go invite them to watch the takeoff?"

"Good idea!" Eddie scrambled down the barn roof and raced to the house, where he asked his mother and father if they would like to see us test a plane we had built out behind the barn. They said sure, they'd be right out. No doubt they were relieved to learn that Eddie was doing something sensible for a change, instead of getting involved in one of the crazy, dangerous schemes he was always coming up with.

When Eddie returned, I was already seated in the rear cockpit. "I thought you would like to be pilot on the first flight," I told him. I doubt that I had ever heard that the rear of an airplane is safer in the event of a crash, but my years of associating with Eddie had given me certain useful intuitions.

About then his parents, strolling arm-in-arm, appeared far down below in the barnyard. They stopped and looked around for the plane their son had built.

"Mom! Dad!" yelled Crazy Eddie. "Up here!"

Mr. and Mrs. Muldoon looked up. Both seemed momentarily paralyzed. Mr. Muldoon's jaw worked up and down, but no words seemed to come out. Mrs. Muldoon sagged against her husband. It was apparent that both of them were overcome with awe by the aeronautical feat accomplished by their only child and his friend.

"Contact!" I yelled.

"Roger!" Crazy Eddie yelled back, giving his parents a jaunty salute.

Mr. Muldoon yelled something, too, but we couldn't make it out, because Eddie had already jerked loose the knot and the wind was rushing in our ears.

Our flight plan worked out just as we had intended. Oh, at first there was some shrill screeching from down below and I had the vague impression of cows leaping fences and trying to climb trees and terrified chickens and geese raising a terrible ruckus, but then the bush plane hit the ramp on the shed roof and we were lofted high into the air. The wind caught us and carried us even higher, and it was wonderful. Far down below we could see tiny houses and horses and cows in the patchwork fields and miniature farmers waving to us from miniature tractors, and there was Sand Creek, like an embroidered line of green and blue meandering through the countryside, and then we soared higher still and were in the clouds, white puffs of vapor floating up like cotton candy, and it was all very lovely and exciting, except I had this pain in my body, and my head ached.

When I opened my eyes, Mr. and Mrs. Muldoon were bent over me, both of them strangely white of face. They were blurred, too, but because their surroundings were in sharp focus, I determined it was because of their shaking.

"Are you all right?" Mrs. Muldoon asked, wringing a stream of perspiration from her hands.

"Yeah, I guess so," I said, propping myself up on an elbow. There was a manure pile nearby and on top of it a pile of kindling and two wagon wheels. Mr. Muldoon said the manure pile had probably saved our lives.

Not too bad, I thought. Any old bush pilot could land on a gravel bar or a little clearing in the forest, but I'd like to see one of them land on a manure pile and live to tell about it.

Both Crazy Eddie and I recovered quickly. In fact, the only lasting ill effect of the bush-plane flight was that the Muldoon cows walked around for weeks afterward with their heads turned to the sky, as if expecting some assault from outer space. Crazy Eddie and I used to chuckle at them while we were building the submarine.

Share and
Share Alike

The sharing of a single big-game animal between two hunters is at once the most delicate and the most complex problem encountered in hunting, with the possible exception of deciding whose vehicle to drive on the hunt. It may be useful to examine the problem in some detail.

Let us begin with a hypothetical situation. As is well known, an elk that is shot dead within fifteen feet of your hunting vehicle will still pull himself together enough to gallop to the very bottom of the steepest canyon within five miles. This is known as the elk's revenge. Assume you have just shot such an elk. You and your hunting partner, whom we'll call Bob, have tracked the elk to the bottom of the canyon. As you stand over the massive form of the felled but still magnificent animal, you become contemplative. One of the things you contemplate is how much bigger an elk is at the bottom of a canyon than it is fifteen feet from your vehicle. (Scientists have calculated that a wounded elk will add fifty pounds to its weight for every hundred yards it gallops down into a canyon.) You now ask yourself two questions: (1) How are you going to lug the elk back up to your vehicle? and (2) Why didn't you go golfing today instead of hunting?

With three round trips each, you and Bob manage to pack out the elk section by section. Neither of you experiences any extraordinary ill effects from the exertion, other than the seizing up of major portions of your cardiovascular systems. Bob lies wheezing by the side of the road, a haunch of elk still strapped to his back. You are walking around on your knees and mumbling about "getting in shape" and not caring if you "never see another *bleeping* elk." At this point you are willing to give the entire elk to Bob, provided that he lives. Your intimate association with elk meat over the preceding hours has diminished your appetite for the stuff and has resulted in a psychological malfunction known as excessive generosity. Wisely, you put off the decision of what share of the elk should go to Bob until you are rested and your mind has cleared.

The culinary aspects of elk meat improve in direct proportion to distance in time from the packing-out process. A week after the hunt, during which time the elk has been aging nicely in a cooler, the thought of all those steaks and roasts stashed away for the winter is intensely satisfying. There is still the problem of what portion of the elk should be Bob's share. You are now in the proper frame of mind to make this decision.

Your reasoning goes something like this: For openers, you consider giving Bob half the elk. Once you have enjoyed a few moments of mirth over this ridiculous notion, you get down to serious figuring. Using half an elk as base, you deduct from it five pounds for each day remaining in the elk season, days in which Bob might very well shoot his own elk. You make further deductions for the amount of whining Bob did while packing out your elk. Then there is the matter of that unseemly phrase Bob blurted out when he learned the elk you had shot was at the bottom of a three-thousand-foot canyon—more deductions, all of them choice cuts. You don't forget Bob's tripping over a log and cartwheeling down the slope with a hindquarter strapped to his packboard. That bruised a lot of meat, some of which was elk. Further deductions. When you finally total the figures, you discover that Bob now owes you approximately one quarter of an elk. The charlatan hasn't even had the courtesy to mention the matter of this debt to you. And to think you trusted him enough to let him help pack your elk out of a three-thousand-foot canyon! Some gratitude!

In the end, your calculations are for naught. Your spouse demands that you give Bob a generous share of the elk. You acquiesce reluctantly but eventually conclude she was right—although this conclusion does not arrive until the middle of April, when even the thought of one more elk roast blights your day.

"What's for supper?" you ask your wife.

"Elk," she replies.

"*Aaaack!*" you say. "How about TV dinners? I'm sick of elk!"

"You shot it, you eat it!"

"I know, I'll call Bob. He would probably like some more elk."

"Are you kidding?" Bob responds. "I'm fed up to

my follicles with elk! I couldn't choke down another bite
of elk if I lived to be five hundred!"

"Oh yes you can and you are! You didn't take your
full share of the elk! You packed it out and you're going
to eat it!"

In this way, the problem of sharing a single big-
game animal between hunters usually resolves itself.

My first encounter with the problem of sharing a
big-game animal occurred when I was sixteen. I was
hunting with my cousin, Buck, who was several years
older than I. At that time, Buck was at the height of his
intellectual powers and knew all there was to know about
hunting and most of everything else. Some people are
stingy with their knowledge and try to hoard it, but not
Buck. He handed his out freely and voluminously and
endlessly, at all hours of the day or night, whether one
was in the market for knowledge or not. Naturally, because of his towering intellect and absolute knowledge
of all matters pertaining to hunting, Buck got to devise
our field tactics.

Shortly after dawn, as Buck was bathing my semi-
consciousness with a steady stream of his hunting knowledge, I glanced up the side of the mountain to clear the
glaze from my eyes and spotted five specks. The specks
were moving.

"Buck, there's a herd of mule deer up there!" I
shouted.

Since part of Buck's knowledge consisted of the
natural law that he was the only one who could spot deer
first, he dismissed my report with a chuckle and the
comment that the specks I saw were probably on my
glasses.

Then he stopped the car and got out, casually, as

if to stretch and satisfy a need for a breath of fresh air. He got back in the car, shook a cigarette from a pack, lit it, blew out the match. "There's a herd of mule deer about halfway up the mountain," he said. "When you're driving out to hunt mule deer, it's a good idea to stop every once in a while and check the slopes. Now you take these deer here, we might have missed them if I hadn't stopped for a look around."

"Good, Buck, good. I'll try to remember that."

Buck then laid out the tactics. "Now here's what we're going to do. You work your way up the mountain toward the deer. I'll drive around to the top of the mountain and wait on the road just in case they try to cut back over the ridge."

"Why don't you climb the mountain and I drive around on the road?"

"Because it wouldn't work, that's why. Besides, if the deer cut back over the ridge, we want to have the best shot to be waiting there."

"Oh."

I got out to start working my way up the mountain, and Buck drove off, leisurely smoking his cigarette and fiddling with the radio dials. There was about a foot of new snow on the mountain, and the climb was cold, slippery, and exhausting. Occasionally a fir tree would unload a bough of snow down the back of my neck, and that didn't improve my mood, either. Nor did the thought of Buck sitting in the warm car at the top of the mountain, drinking hot coffee from the thermos and smoking and listening to the radio, while he gave the deer time to detect my presence and then retreat practically into his lap.

But it didn't work out that way. All at once I found

myself right in the middle of the herd of mule deer. A nice little buck stepped from behind a tree and stared at me, as if astonished to find a human being stupid enough to be climbing a snow-covered mountain that early in the morning. I downed him with a single shot. The rest of the herd raced off in all directions, except toward Buck. An hour later I was back down on the road with my deer. Buck, who had witnessed the "whole fiasco," as he called it, was waiting for me. He was hot, too.

"Boy, that was dumb!" he snarled. "Shooting that itty-bitty buck when there was one three times as big in the herd. I knew I shouldn't give you the best chance, but since you're just a kid and all, I thought I'd do you the favor. Boy, did you blow it!"

We rode in silence all the way home, Buck occupied with what I could easily guess were dire thoughts, and I, with gloating. When you're sixteen and wear glasses and aren't that good at sports and spend a good deal of time in the company of an intellectual giant, you don't get much opportunity for gloating. When you do, you savor it.

"You just remember," Buck said, after dropping me and my deer off home, "part of that deer is mine."

When I got around to cutting up the deer, I at first considered giving Buck a full half of it. On the other hand, I had my mother, grandmother, and sister to provide wild game for, and Buck lived by himself in an apartment. If he tried to eat half a deer all by himself, he would soon become sick of venison and wouldn't want to go deer hunting ever again. No, I told myself, it would be better if I gave him only a hindquarter. That would be about right for one person.

On the other hand, steaks cut from the hindquarter of a deer are awfully good eating. Buck might use a venison-steak dinner as bait to lure one of his girl friends into his apartment. That in all probability could lead to Buck and the girl committing a serious sin. Since my religion forbade even contributing to serious sin, I was not about to risk going to hell over a hindquarter of venison. No sir, Buck would have to make do with a front quarter.

But which front quarter? That presented no real difficulty. Because of Buck's interest in science, he would be intrigued by studying the effect of a .30/30 slug on the shoulder of a deer. There was still a lot of good meat on the shoulder, too.

Upon further consideration, I decided that Buck might prefer to forgo his scientific studies and have the shoulder ground up into venison burger. So I ground up the venison for him.

Well, that turned out to be an awful lot of venison burger for one person. I started dividing it up into neat little piles, until I found the exact amount that I thought would be suitable for Buck. I then left his share on the table while I went to deposit the rest of the venison in the cold storage locker.

A few days later I ran into Buck. "Hey, you little rat," he greeted me, "where's my share of our deer?"

I shook my head sadly. "You may have some trouble believing this, Buck, but while I was taking my share down to the locker, the cat got in the house and ate your share."

Buck did not take the news well.

Never Sniff
a Gift Fish

There is one thing about my neighbor Al Finley that irritates me. Well, actually, there are many things about Finley that irritate me, but one stands out from the others. It is his constant seeking after immortality.

I don't mean to say that Finley wants to live forever, although he probably has that in mind, too. And if the population of the world should one day increase to the point where people are standing on each other's shoulders, you can bet Finley won't be one of the guys on the bottom. No, he will be up on top, shouting orders to the fellow down below to step along faster and watch out for the bumps. That's the sort of person Finley is.

On the off chance he doesn't achieve immortality for his person, Finley at least wants it for his name. He is driven by this ambition.

For a while, he thought he might achieve lasting fame by writing poetry. When his masterwork, "Ode to a Liver Spot," brought him bad reviews and several threats against his life, he decided he might stand a better chance of achieving immortality in the sciences. His anti-gravitational device worked but once—when his wife stepped on it while cleaning the basement—and it worked then only because she thought it was something that had crawled out from behind the furnace.

After reading a book on Disraeli, Finley decided he was destined to become a great statesman. He won a seat on the city council and quickly became a master of political acrobatics. He now straddles fences, juggles books, and can change horses in midstream without rocking the boat. Nevertheless, it appears that he will not rise above the level of city councilman, which is a good sign that the system works.

Despite Finley's pitiful failures at achieving immortality, he continues to pursue his quarry, like an untrained pup let loose in the fields, to whom every grasshopper is a rabbit in disguise. His most recent quest for lasting fame took shape on a fishing trip with Retch Sweeney and me.

Retch and I honked Finley out of bed at four-thirty in the morning. He staggered out to the car, his gear in his arms, and muttered, "This is an ungodly hour to wake a man!"

"Early to bed, early to rise, makes a man healthy, wealthy, and wise," I replied.

"The early bird gets the worm," said Retch, chortling.

Finley's face brightened. "Who said that?"

"We did," said Retch. "You see anybody else in the car?"

"He means who said it first," I explained to Retch. "Those famous quotations are probably both from Ben

Franklin. Old Ben thought up about ninety-eight percent of all the famous quotations."

"I thought he invented kites," Retch said.

I could only shake my head in disgust. For a man
with sixteen years of education, Retch was surprisingly
ignorant. True, all sixteen years were spent in grade
school, but he should have learned something.

Finley had turned thoughtful, as he does whenever
he is contemplating his own immortality. "You know,"
he said, "Ben Franklin is probably remembered as much
for his sayings as he is for his inventions. But have you
ever noticed how few famous sayings have been derived
from the outdoor sports?"

"Now that you mention it, I can only think of a
couple," I replied. "There are the ones about a bird in
hand being worth two in the bush and a miss being as
good as a mile. That's all I can think of. Anyway, probably the reason there are so few famous quotations derived from the outdoor sports is that old Ben was primarily
an indoor sport."

"You know," Finley mused aloud, "I bet that a person who thought up a lot of quotations related to the
outdoor sports could practically achieve, uh, immortality."

I was instantly sorry the subject had ever come up
and tried to change it by asking Retch if he had found
another dry fly like the one he'd had such great luck
with the previous weekend. He said he hadn't and was
darn sorry to have lost the fly before having a chance
to tie up some duplicates.

Finley, who had continued musing in the back seat,
injected himself into the conversation. "For want of a
fly, the fish is lost," he said.

Putting our lives at risk, for I was driving, I twisted

around in the seat to turn the full force of my glare on Finley. "That's horrible," I cried. "That is truly disgusting!"

"Curve! Curve!" Retch shouted.

"You stay out of this," I snapped. "This is between Finley and me."

"I thought it was pretty good," Finley said. "People probably didn't care much for Ben Franklin's 'early to rise' quote when they first heard it either."

"Truck! Truck!" cried Retch, obviously trying to distract me from giving Finley the tongue-lashing he deserved.

"You can't just think up famous sayings," I told Finley. "It doesn't work that way. Anybody knows that."

"Why not?" said Finley. "Somebody has to think them up."

"Train! Train!" yelled Retch.

I could tell I wasn't going to win any argument with Finley, particularly with Retch clowning around, so I calmed my nerves by concentrating totally on driving. I had seen men before who didn't know how to control their nerves. Retch Sweeney was one of them. Even while driving out for a little fishing and relaxation, he was all pale and twitchy and had even twisted his cap up into a knot. I think he drinks too much coffee.

"Never sniff a gift fish," said Finley.

I could see then that the situation was hopeless. We would just have to let Finley's malady run its course.

"Get it?" Finley continued. "That means you shouldn't be too critical of something that's given to you."

I told him I thought that bit of wisdom had been covered by gift horses.

"But how many gift horses have you received lately?"

Finley asked, smirking. "That's right, none. Now, a gift fish, that's a lot more common and people would identify with it."

"Well, I'd certainly sniff any fish you gave me, that's for sure," I told him.

Finley was quiet all the rest of the way to the river. I thought maybe I had hurt his feelings and discouraged him from thinking up more famous quotations. Unfortunately, that wasn't the case. The case was that thinking up famous quotations is more difficult than one might expect.

We set up camp and spent the rest of the day fishing, or, more accurately, practicing our fly casting. Toward evening we picked up a couple of smallish rainbows, which would have been enough for supper with a couple of gift fish thrown in. We drew straws for the trout, and Finley and I had to settle for a supper of canned hash. We set two plates of hash out on a log, ostensibly to cool but actually to let the darkness build up a bit. I knew a man once who tried to eat some canned hash in broad daylight, but his jaw froze up on him and had to be pried open with a spoon. Ever since then I have waited until dark to eat my hash. When the night was ripe enough, I dug in, giving a little shout before each bite to give any insect life a chance to escape. I explained to Finley that this was one of the lesser-known bits of woodlore I had picked up over the years.

"Yes," he said, "two bugs in the hash are worth one in the mouth."

"There's some truth to that one," I said, "but it's not particularly memorable."

"How about this one?" Retch put in. "When all the straws are the same length, the man that holds 'em gets to eat the fish! Har!"

Finley and I stared at him. "Now I've got one," I said. "The man who cheats his fishing partners had better learn to sleep lightly!"

"Listen, you guys, I was only kidding," Retch said, nervously. "I got the short straw! It wasn't *real* short, but it was short."

"The man who lies to his fishing partners may wake up with hash in his boots," said Finley.

"I like that one," I said. "It's the sort of famous quotation I can remember."

It was a mistake to offer Finley encouragement. As we lay in our sleeping bags, Retch and I trying to get to sleep, Finley ran off one freshly minted famous outdoor quotation after another:

"The pessimist complains that he just lost a lunker and the optimist brags he just had a great strike.

"What the tourist terms a plague of insects, the fisherman calls a fine hatch.

"No fisherman ever bragged that the huge fish he hooked turned out to be a log.

"What do you think of those?" he asked.

"Shut up and go to sleep is what I think of them," I growled. "Or to put it another way, how would you like a sock in the mouth?"

"All that's gruff isn't tough. Say, that's a pretty good *umph aggh muff*—"

It wasn't one of my clean socks, either.

The next day there was no holding Finley back. From way off down the stream, he shouted at Retch and me, "I got one! I got one!" Naturally, Retch and I rushed off toward him.

When we arrived, too late it appeared, Finley was standing there sorting through his fly box.

"Did you—*puff puff*—lose it?" I asked.

He looked up and smiled. "A man who fishes in sneakers never gets in over the top of his waders."

"Wha . . . ?"

"You've got to admit that's a pretty good one," he said.

"So, where's the fish?" Retch gasped, his mental agility having peaked at age six.

"There is no fish," I explained, plucking a section of devil's club from my armpit. "There is only another famous outdoor quotation."

Retch removed a small pine cone from his ear. "Listen, we could say he wandered off into the woods and disappeared. Nobody would know, nobody would care!"

Finley calmly tied on a fly and made a dismal cast that fell a good ten feet short of the pool he was aiming for. Inexplicably, a nice rainbow glommed the fly.

"A cast that reaches a fish is never too short," he said smugly. "I'd better write that one down."

Retch and I knew we were beaten and wandered off downstream. "Geez," Retch muttered. "If famous quotations were fish, he'd be over his limit by now."

"Don't you start!" I said.

"What?"

"Nothing."

On the drive back home, Finley was fairly spewing with famous outdoor quotations:

"The angler who doesn't look before he leaps will have his next cast made of plaster.

"There is no greater fan of fly fishing than the worm.

"I have never met a fish I didn't like.

"Who was that fish I seen you with the other night? That was no fish, that was my muddler.

"Even a fish stick once knew the glories of the deep."

And on and on.

Finally I screamed, "Enough, Finley, enough! You've invented enough famous outdoor quotations to compile your own *Bartlett's*. Henceforth, no angler will give an after-dinner speech without first perusing his *Finley's*. Now stop, before you flood the market."

"But so far I've only covered fishing," he replied. "There's still camping and hiking and boating and, of course, hunting."

"Please, Lord, deliver us!" cried out Retch, who had never before shown much inclination toward religion.

Finley cleared his throat:

"A goose may honk but will not wave.

"It is a foolish hunter who . . ."

Backseats
I Have Known

The backseat of my new compact sedan is so small and cramped we have to grease the children to get them in and out of it. That's what started me thinking recently about the decline of the backseat in American life, about all the wonderful adventures I've had in backseats, about all the backseats I've known and loved.

Among the older readers there are probably those who hold nostalgic recollections of the backseat mainly as the trysting place of young love. Indeed, I remember one such incident in my own steamy, R-rated adolescence.

At age sixteen I had already acquired a reputation as a suave and debonair ladies' man. My first real date, with the scintillating and sizzlingly beautiful Olga Bonemarrow, pretty much established my style as a worldly, dashing young-man-about-town, a person born to the fast lane of life. The only thing that crimped my style was parental reluctance to allow me to get my hands on our new car, a prospect Mom and Hank, my stepfather, equated with an imminent arrival of the apocalypse. Finally, I gave them an ultimatum.

Hank pondered the ultimatum a spell and then said to my mother, "As I understand it, either we let him have the car for a date with Olga Bonemarrow or he runs off and joins the French Foreign Legion and we never see him again. What's it going to be?"

"Don't rush me," Mom said. "I'm still weighing the options."

Eventually, they gave in and let me have the car. I cruised over to Olga's house and picked her up. "Neato!" she said. "What a neat car!"

To get Olga into the proper mood, I took her to a movie, a Randolph Scott western, and afterward blew nearly a whole buck on a double order of hamburgers, malts, and French fries. Then I drove her out to the gravel pit and parked. No dummy, Olga sensed right away that I was up to something.

"Whatcha stop here for?" she asked, giggling coyly.

"I dunno," I said, always quick with a quip. "Say, would you look at that pile of gravel!"

"Neato," Olga said.

We sat there without talking for a while, listening to the radio and staring out at the pile of gravel. Then, very cool and casual, I made a suggestion.

"Say, Olga," I said, "how'd you like to get into the backseat? It's real nice back there."

Olga giggled. "Neato," she said, her voice going low and husky, her lovely, thick eyelashes fluttering like a duet of moths. Nevertheless, there was something about her response that made me uneasy. Perhaps it was the way she took out her wad of bubble gum and stuck it on the gearshift knob before vaulting into the backseat.

So there we were, with Gene Autry crooning softly on the airwaves and the light of a full moon illuminating the sensuous curves of the highway department's gravel pile. I let the mood build, then asked suavely, "How do you like it back there? Lots of leg room, ain't there?"

"Yeah, neato," she said, icing up the windows. "Guess what, I just remembered, my folks were expecting me home a half hour ago."

Perhaps I was too wild and impetuous for Olga, or so I gathered from the fact that it was nearly six months before she again acknowledged my existence. In any case, I had learned a good lesson, namely that there are some women who just don't like to live life in the fast lane.

The Olga episode aside, my love affair with the backseat has nothing to do with romance or other such nonsense but with the great outdoors. Nowadays, when almost every outdoorsman owns a van, a camper, a trailer, or a motor home, only we old-timers recall that the predecessor of these conveyances was the backseat. The backseat of his car could provide an outdoorsman with emergency shelter, a bed for the night if need be; it was his gun and rod rack, his larder, tool chest, survival kit, closet; his sanctuary from mosquitoes, gnats, and strange sounds in the night; his garbage dump, woodshed, storage room, tackle box, and more. The test of an outdoorsman in the old days was his ability to find in his backseat whatever he needed to survive in the back-road wilds of America.

"We're done for now," his partner might say. "There's a big tree across the road."

The outdoorsman would shrug and reply: "Not for long. I got a chain saw, a peavey, two splitting wedges, a maul, and a double-bitted ax in the backseat."

In those days, a man needed only three things to survive for months in the outdoors: a gun, a good knife, and a properly outfitted backseat.

The backseat was not without its dangers. Retch Sweeney and I once ate for two days on a bag of jerky he found in a corner of his backseat. It wasn't great jerky or even good but still moderately edible, at least until Retch recalled that he had never put any jerky in his backseat.

"Well, if it isn't jerky, what is it?" I asked.

"I don't want to talk about it," Retch said greenly.

Another time, as Retch and I were rounding a curve on a steep mountain road, an avalanche swept down from out of my backseat and engulfed us. Somehow, I managed to bring the car to a stop and dig myself out. Then I went around to the other side of the car and probed the jumbled mass of camp gear with a stick until I found Retch, and just in the nick of time, too. Fortunately, his face was in a small pocket of air between a boot and a coffee pot, and he had been able to breathe. The air probably would have given out, though, if I had had to bring in specially trained search-and-rescue dogs to find him.

Another danger of backseats was that methane gas sometimes arose from decay in the bottom layers. For that reason, most experienced outdoorsmen never allowed an open flame inside the car, particularly after an outing lasting more than three days.

Retch's wife once accidentally opened a rear door of his camping car and later was found crouched in a corner of the garage, whimpering and sucking her thumb. The doctor sent her to bed under heavy sedation. He said he thought she was suffering from a psychosis of some kind. I think it was probably from a string of crappies mislaid in the backseat on a fishing trip the previous July.

I have long thought that a good horror movie could be made about the backseat of a hunter's car. These two hunters are driving along way back in the mountains on a dark and stormy night, see, and suddenly the backseat begins to pulsate. Slowly it begins to ooze forward, toward the necks of the unsuspecting hunters. At the end of the film a posse with a pack of dogs pursues the backseat into a swamp where it slips beneath the greenish ooze, burbling evilly. Retch scoffed at my idea.

I was miffed. "Listen," I told him, "I know for a fact a strange life form can originate in a backseat."

"Let's not get personal," he snapped.

There is a science to packing a backseat prior to a camping trip. Unfortunately, no one has ever discovered a suitable method for repacking it for the return trip. This is because camp gear during the course of the trip expands to half again its original volume and overflows into the front seat. On the way home from one camping trip, I was stopped by a traffic cop who claimed he thought the car was being driven by a water jug and a half-inflated air mattress.

Another reason that repacking the backseat poses problems is that the process always takes place during a thunderous rainstorm. The prescribed method of packing a backseat under that circumstance is to hurl the entire camp blindly and savagely through a rear door of the car. One time we came home from a Forest Service campground with a pine branch, several large rocks, a rest room sign, and a ranger who had stopped by to collect the fee.

One of the most efficient repackings of a backseat I've ever seen was accomplished by Retch's father when we were boys. Mr. Sweeney hated the outdoors and everything in it, but once, during a mellowness brought on by a quart of home brew, he promised to drive little Retch and me out for an overnighter. His wife held him to the promise. Grousing and grumbling, he drove Retch and me out to the first wide spot in the road, which happened to be a logging camp garbage dump. Retch and I set up the tent and stowed the gear in it while Mr. Sweeney sat in the car, frowning at his newspaper. Along about sundown, as Retch and I were frying supper, we looked up to see bears of all sizes, shapes, and colors streaming toward our camp. It was a startling sight, to which Mr. Sweeney responded with the quaint expression, "What the *bleep!*" He screamed at us to get in the car. Then he wrapped his arms around the umbrella tent, ripped it from its moorings, dragged it complete with contents to the car, and rammed, crammed, and stomped it into the backseat, all the while helping Retch and me expand our vocabularies. I was too shaken up to time him, but I doubt that more than eight seconds elapsed between our spotting the bears and our careening out of the dump at 60 m.p.h. It was a remarkable performance.

Sleeping in a backseat can be something of an art. As much gear as possible is moved to the front seat and the rest is thrown out on the ground to be repacked during a thunderous rainstorm the next day. Then you roll out your sleeping bag and climb into it. Because this step takes half the night, it should be begun early. Next, you tangle your hair, if any, in the door handle; this will prevent you from rolling onto the floor, which can be disastrous, particularly to the other parties who may be sleeping in the backseat with you. (Yes, it is entirely possible for more than one outdoorsman at a time to sleep in a backseat; however, check with your doctor, your minister, and the local health department before attempting to do so.)

I once spent a night sleeping in a backseat with two other guys, but never again. The next morning we got up, built a fire, cooked and ate breakfast, and hunted for two hours before we got completely untangled.

The backseat was, I suppose, as much a state of mind as anything. It was a symbol of freedom and adventure. It was the pioneer's Conestoga wagon shrunk down and upholstered; it was the prospector's burro with ashtrays and armrests. Then one day, I judge about the late fifties, some guy, a genius, probably an outdoorsman who had just spent the night sleeping in a backseat, came up with a fantastic idea: Suppose a vehicle could be built that was nothing more than a huge backseat equipped with engine and wheels! The motor home was born.

Edgy Rider

As a child I constantly begged my father to buy me a pony. One day I extracted from him the promise that if he saw an inexpensive steed at the auction he would buy it for me. He came home with a pig.

"Where's my pony?" I demanded.

He pointed to the pig. "You're lookin' at it."

I named the pig Trigger.

Naturally, I was enraged. Other farm kids had their own ponies to gallop about on while I had to ride a stupid pig! On the pig's behalf, I'll say that he cared as much for being ridden as I did for riding him.

"Whoa, Trigger!" I'd scream at the pig.

"Oink oink squeeeeeeeeee!" he'd reply, and race along a barbwire fence in an attempt to saw me into four equal sections.

The great humiliation, though, was when my pony-owning friends would come over to play cowboys. The only one who sat short in the saddle, I always had to be the villain. "Hey, Podner," one of the guys would say to his sidekick, "I think ol' Black Bart is trying to sneak up on us—I just heard his horse oink!" Then they'd laugh.

That fall I had little trouble containing my grief when Trigger was transformed into hams and salt pork. Seldom does one have the opportunity of eating an adversary without being subjected to criticism. Nevertheless, I was still without a suitable steed.

Crazy Eddie Muldoon, who lived on a nearby farm and was also horseless, came up with the theory that cows might be employed as satisfactory mounts. The theory seemed reasonable enough to me, as any wild scheme did in those days, and I agreed to help him test it.

"Since it's my idea, I'll do the hard part," explained Crazy Eddie. "That means you get to ride the cow first and have all the fun."

This seemed uncharacteristically generous of him, and I inquired as to the exact nature of the "hard part." He said it consisted of studying the results of the experiment and thinking up ways by which the ride might be improved upon. "And I have to keep a watch out for Pa, too," he concluded. "He's down working in the bottom pasture right now. But we don't want him showing up while you're riding the cow. Understand?"

I understood. Mr. Muldoon was a burly Irishman with a volcanic temper, and he strongly objected to scientific experiments being conducted on his livestock.

Getting on board a cow turned out to be more difficult than either of us had supposed. Crazy Eddie would try to boost me up, but the cow would give us an indignant look and walk away, with me clawing at her hide and Eddie running along grunting and gasping and trying to shove me topside. Finally, he said he had another idea, which was that I would climb up on a shed roof overhanging the barnyard and, when he drove a cow past, I would drop down on her back.

"And presto!" he exclaimed obscurely.

As soon as I was perched on the edge of the roof, Crazy Eddie cut out from the herd a huge Holstein, one approximately the size of a Sherman tank, and drove her unsuspectingly beneath my perch. According to plan, I dropped down on the cow's broad back, grabbing her bell collar as I landed. And presto! The Holstein emitted a terrified bellow, leaped straight up in the air, and executed a rolling figure eight with full twist. That was for openers, a little warmup exercise to get out the kinks and limber up her muscles. Then she stretched out like a greyhound after a mechanical rabbit and did four three-second laps around the barnyard, a maneuver apparently intended to build momentum for a straight shot down the narrow lane behind the barn.

With hands locked like sweating visegrips around the bell collar, and every toe gripping cowhide, I stuck to the back of the Holstein like a hungry, sixty-five-pound bobcat, which may have been exactly what the cow thought I was. During the first moments of my ride, I wondered vaguely if Mr. Muldoon's cows were equipped with burglar alarms, for there was a terrible din in my ears; only later did I attribute this fierce clanging to the cowbell.

About midway down the lane, I managed to unlatch my eyelids—a mistake, as I instantly realized, for the first thing I saw was a compounding of my troubles. There, plodding up the lane toward us, possibly with nothing more on his mind than the question of what his wife had fixed for lunch, was Mr. Muldoon. Now, unknown to me, the barnyard antics of the Holstein had terrorized the rest of the herd, which was stampeding along immediately behind us. It was this wild and violent spectacle that greeted Mr. Muldoon as he glanced up from his preoccupation with picking his way through patches of cow spoor laid down with the singular indiscrimination for which cows are noted. In retrospect, this preoccupation bore a certain similarity to concern about a few drops of rain just before one falls in a lake.

Overcoming the momentary paralysis that accompanied his first sight of us, Mr. Muldoon exploded into furious activity, which consisted largely of jumping up and down and waving his arms. The clanging of the burglar-alarm cowbell prevented me from hearing what he was shouting, which was probably just as well. Perceiving that his efforts to flag down the herd were not only ineffective but, if anything, were increasing the cows' RPMs, Mr. Muldoon turned and began to sprint ahead of us at a rate that under normal circumstances I'm sure I would have marveled at. As it was, we passed over him as if he were a tansy weed rooted in the ground.

My dismount from the Holstein was facilitated by a low-hanging limb on a tree at the end of the lane. I bounced several times, finally coming to rest in a posture similar to that associated with a lump of mush. Fortunately, I had landed beyond the exit of the lane, and the herd of cows that thundered close behind showed the good sportsmanship of fanning out on both sides of me. Mr. Muldoon had not been so lucky. When he came hobbling up to see if I was still alive, I noted that he appeared to have been pressed in a giant waffle iron, and one none too clean at that. I choked out the story of the experiment to him, and he showed considerable interest in it, mentioning in passing that he could scarcely wait to debrief Eddie in the woodshed. Crazy Eddie, I might add, was at that very moment in the house busting open his piggy bank to see if he had enough money for a bus ticket to another state. I was happy to learn that he came up short by several dollars.

My craving for a suitable mount, by which I mean one that did not go *oink* or *moo,* was never to be satisfied.

Years later, my own children began begging me for a horse. At the time, we lived in one of the humbler sections of suburbia, an area which, through some oversight of the planning commission, remained zoned for agriculture. This meant that it was legally possible for us to keep a horse on our two acres. I decided to broach the subject to my wife.

"I've been thinking," I broached, "every kid should have a horse. Caring for a horse gives a kid a sense of responsibility."

"What do you need a horse for?" Bun replied. "You already have a four-wheel-drive pickup with racing stripes and a chrome rollbar."

That woman can be incredibly dense at times. "Not for me! Ha! I can just see myself, dressed up like Clint Eastwood in *High Plains Drifter,* galloping off into the sunset!" Actually, I didn't look bad that way, not bad at all, but I wasn't about to give Bun the satisfaction of thinking she'd had one of her suspicions confirmed. "Yes, by gosh, I think we should buy the kids a horse."

"But we don't even have a barn!" Bun wailed.

"We can turn the garage into a barn," I explained. "Listen, all we need is a little imagination."

"All you need is a good psychiatrist," she muttered.

Later, when I was copping a plea of temporary insanity, I would remind her of that mutter.

Contrary to popular opinion, it is remarkably easy to buy a horse, but only if you know absolutely nothing about horses. I found an ad in the classified section of the newspaper that stated: "Good kids' horse, $150." It seemed like a steal. Surely, I thought, at this very moment hordes of eager horse buyers are converging upon the foolish soul who is offering such a fantastic bargain. I dialed the number, and the man who answered—he spoke in the soft, country drawl I had expected—confirmed that indeed he was all but overrun with potential buyers.

"I don't want to sell Pokey to just anyone, though," he told me. "Since you sound like a man who knows horses, I'd be happy to bring him by your place so you can take a look at him."

I said I'd be delighted if he would do that and gave him the address of my spread. Scarcely had I hung up the phone than an old pickup truck with a horse in the back came rattling down my driveway.

A lanky cowboy emerged from the cab of the pickup. Extending a hard-callused hand, he said, "Name's Bill. You the man what's lookin' for a good kids' horse?"

I replied that I was indeed that person. By this time, my brood of moppets were bouncing up and down around me, clapping their little hands together, and screaming, "Buy him! Buy him!"

"Hush," I scolded them. "I'm going to have to have a closer look at him first."

"Sure thing," Bill said. He dropped the tailgate of the pickup and ordered the horse, "Step out of there,

Pokey." Amazingly, the horse backed up and stepped down out of the pickup. Then the cowboy scooped up our little three-year-old and set her on Pokey's back. I'll swear that horse turned and smiled affectionately at Erin. He walked ever so carefully around the yard, stopping every time she teetered one way or the other until the little girl recovered her balance, and then he'd plod on.

My wife, who was witnessing the performance, also seemed impressed with the horse's gentleness, or so I judged from the fact that she had ceased pounding her chest in an apparent effort to get her heart started again.

"What'd I tell you," Bill said. "Pokey's a great kids' horse."

There was no doubt about it. While Bill was lifting Erin back down, I was writing out the check. Perhaps I wouldn't have been so hasty if I'd had the good sense to study the horse's face more carefully. When I finally did so, I had the distinct impression that it bore a combination of features that reminded me of W. C. Fields and, in a different mood, of Richard Widmark in one of his roles as a homicidal maniac. Probably just my imagination, though, I said to myself.

One little incident before Bill departed also caused me some wonder about my purchase. As Bill was wringing my hand as though I had just saved his life, Pokey plodded softly up behind him. I assumed the horse was going to give his former master an affectionate good-bye nudge. Instead, he clamped half a dozen yellow teeth onto the cowboy's shoulder. I recall the smirking look in the horse's eyes as Bill danced about, silently mouthing curses as he reached back and twisted one of Pokey's ears until the animal unlocked its jaws. Bill grinned sheepishly, if you can imagine the grin of a sheep that

has just been gnawed on by a coyote. "A little game
Pokey and I play," he said.

"Really?" I said. "I would have guessed that hurt
like heck."

Bill casually flicked a tear off his cheek. "Naw! Heck
no. Well, be seein' you."

Contrary to his last remark, I never saw Bill again.
But I can say in all honesty, I really would have liked
to, and preferably in some remote area where his shouts
for help would have been to no avail.

Within a month, I could not look at Pokey without
seeing "glue factory" written all over him. The only thing
that saved him from taking up residence on the back
side of postage stamps was that the children loved him.
And, as far as I could determine, he loved the children.
He lived with us for ten years, providing the children
with almost as much pleasure as he did the tack-shop
owner, the feedstore proprietor, the farrier, and the
veterinarian. I viewed him largely as a malevolent machine for transforming five-dollar bills into fertilizer for
my garden.

I must admit that I had some ulterior motives in
acquiring a horse. My wife's charges that I intended to
satisfy the cowboy fantasies of my childhood were, of
course, too ridiculous to dignify even with denial. I did
think, however, that the horse might come in handy for
elk hunting, so I went out and purchased some of the
essential gear for that purpose.

Bun knows nothing about elk hunting, but even so
I thought her response to my acquisitions was uncouth,
to say the least. Personally, I find it unladylike for a
woman to stagger about holding her sides while squeal-
ing hysterically.

"Laugh all you want," I told her, "but if you weren't so ignorant of the subject you'd know that nine out of ten elk hunters wear cowboy hats. Cowboy boots are the only safe footwear for stirrups—anybody knows that. And the brush on the sides of trails will tear your legs to pieces if you don't have a good pair of chaps. The leather vest—well, you'd just be surprised at how handy a leather vest is when you're hunting elk!"

"B-but the spurs!" she gasped. "The sp-spurs!"

I didn't even try to explain the spurs. I mean, if a woman is so ignorant of elk hunting that she doesn't know about spurs, there's no point in trying to educate her.

It had been twenty years and more since I had ridden a horse, or a pig or cow for that matter, so before embarking on Pokey myself I considered it only prudent to study the horse's style while the children rode him about the two acres I now referred to in taverns as the "back forty." With the older children, he would gallop at a moderate gait around the fenced pasture, slowing for the corners and in general taking every precaution not to unseat the young riders. Several knowledgeable horsepersons who observed him thus in action told me I couldn't have found a better kids' horse. I would nod knowingly, chewing on a grass straw as I pushed my cowboy hat back with my thumb.

One day when the kids were off at school, I told Bun, "I think I'll take a little ride on Pokey, just to shape him up for elk season."

"I was wondering why you had your chaps on," she said. "Where are your—*hee! hee!*—spurs?"

"The spurs are for later," I said, ignoring her mirthful outburst. "Now, come on out to the back forty with me. I may need some assistance."

"Okay," she agreed, "but if you think I'm going elk hunting with you to help you get on and off your horse, you're crazy."

Perhaps it was fate that dictated I would have to suffer insults in my pursuit of horsemanship. The problem was, I had not yet been willing to mortgage the house in order to swing financing for a saddle. Since the children mounted the horse by using the board fence as a ladder, I figured I could do the same. This procedure, however, was made easier if someone held the horse's bridle while the mounting was taking place.

Maybe my imagination was acting up, but the expression on Pokey's face that day seemed more Richard Widmark than W. C. Fields. Nevertheless, I climbed the fence and, while Bun maneuvered the horse up close, I threw a leg over him. So far, so good. I took up the reins and told Bun to step back.

"Giddap," I said.

Nothing.

"Giddap!" I said, louder.

Still no response whatsoever. I looked at Bun. She shrugged her shoulders.

"GIDDAP, you miserable *bleep-of-a-bleep!*"

The *bleep-of-a-bleep* lowered his head, against which he had now flattened his ears, but refused to budge.

Once more I shouted "Giddap," but this time I dug my heels into his flanks. Before my hat hit the ground at the starting point, we were at the far end of the back forty. But it was not so simple as that.

The smooth, rhythmic lope with which Pokey carried the children about the pasture had been replaced by a gait closely simulating the motion of a jackhammer—a thousand-pound jackhammer. My eyeglasses flew off, the fillings in my teeth popped loose, my vertebrae rattled like castanets. With the instincts of a natural horseman, I hauled back on the reins. Unfortunately, the motion of the horse had bounced me so far forward, I had to stretch the reins far back behind me, and even then couldn't get the slack out of them. But this problem had ceased to concern me, since I now had another distraction.

For those unfamiliar with a horse's anatomy, there is a large bone at the point where the neck hooks on to the rest of him, technically speaking. I now found myself astraddle this bone, pounding against it at a rate of five times per second. On the scale of discomfort, this sensation rated somewhere between unbearable and unbelievable, thus motivating me to take defensive action. I flopped forward and wrapped both arms around the beast's neck, a move which had the purpose not only of enabling me to hold on but possibly to strangle the horse into submission. Alas, at that moment, Pokey cut sharply around a corner, so that I was swung beneath his neck. We arrived back at the starting point with me suspended from the horse's neck in the manner of a two-toed sloth from a limb. Pokey came to a reluctant halt, and I dropped to the ground. Calmly, I picked up my hat, beat the dust out of it on my chaps, and strolled over to Bun, who was sagged against the fence doing her impression of a limp noodle.

"Want to see any more trick riding?" I asked.

Despite my air of nonchalance, the ride had taken its toll on me. Suddenly, in fact, I detected what I thought was the symptom of a heart attack—an excruciating pain in my shoulder. Then, collecting my wits, I reached back, got hold of an ear, and twisted it until Pokey unclamped his jaws.

Pokey was truly a great kids' horse. But he hated adults.

Our next yard sale included a cowboy hat, cowboy boots, chaps, and a leather vest.

"Don't you want to sell the spurs?" Bun asked.

"No, I'm keeping them," I said, "just in case I ever run into Bill again!"

Strange Scenes
and Eerie Events

Every day weird things happen for which there are no rational explanations. Take, for example, the case of Retch Sweeney's watch.

Retch and I were trolling on a lake in Canada several years ago and, as he leaned over the side of the boat to net a nice rainbow trout I was bringing in, Retch's watch came loose from his wrist and fell into the lake. Not only was the watch expensive, but it held great sentimental value: Retch's wife had given it to him on their twentieth anniversary. It bore the inscription, "To Charley Bombi, for 40 years dedicated service to Acme Sand & Gravel Co." Retch's wife is a great one for sentiment.

Five years after Retch lost his watch in the Canadian lake, he and I went on a boat-camping trip on a lake in Montana. It is important to note that there is no waterway connecting the two lakes. After making camp, Retch and I went out to see if we couldn't hook into one of the monster rainbows reported in the vicinity. Sure enough, as we trolled past the mouth of a stream, Retch's rod whipped double and a few seconds later a beautiful rainbow was doing aerial gymnastics. We went back to camp and while I started preparing supper, Retch dressed out his fish. Suddenly he let out a great yell. I rushed over to see what had happened.

"Look what I found in this rainbow," he shouted, holding up a shiny object.

"I can scarcely believe my eyes," I said. "How could such a thing happen?"

"Beats me," Retch said. "I've never even heard of anybody finding a bottle cap in the stomach of a fish before."

"Me either," I said. "Now if it had been the watch you lost in the lake up in Canada, I could understand that. You read in the newspapers all the time about that sort of thing happening."

Some persons seem to possess almost supernatural powers. One of the ways Retch and I pass the time when the fishing slows down on a lake is to toss a floating ring well out from the boat and then hold casting contests to see who can hit the ring most often. Fred Dokes happened to be along with us one time and he couldn't miss the ring. Retch and I were impressed.

"All right, now I'll really show you something," Fred said. "Something that will amaze you." He took from his pocket a wad of stuff that looked like cookie dough and placed a plug of it over each eye. Next he tied a large bandana over the top of the dough. Finally, he took off his jacket and tied that around his head in such a way that it was absolutely impossible for him to see out, even if he hadn't had the dough over each eye.

"Hand me my rod," he said, standing up in the

boat. "Now what I want you to do is to spin me around five times. You don't need to worry about pointing me in the direction of the floating ring."

I spun him around five times. Naturally, the only thing I expected would happen was that Fred would stagger backwards and fall into the lake.

"Okay, just watch this," he said. Fred then took two steps backwards and fell into the lake.

Of all the people who seem to have supernatural powers, Fred proved that he wasn't one of them. When he offered to show us how he could shoot skeet blind-folded, we declined on the grounds that watching too many demonstrations of extrasensory perception can bring on a nervous condition.

Even weirder was what happened to Retch and me up in the Hoodoo Valley. We had spent the day fishing on a remote lake and had so much fun that it was prac-tically dark before we knew it. Then the wind came up and big black clouds came rolling over the mountains, and the sky was cobwebbed with lightning. We got the boat loaded and headed off down the winding, two-lane highway. Even in the daylight, this highway is spooky but on a dark and stormy night it can really give you the creeps. Mist hangs in tattered shrouds over the swampy land; ancient, moss-draped trees line the road, their branches moaning in the wind, and from time to time dark, shaggy shapes scurry through the beams of the headlights.

Rain began to splatter the windshield before we had driven a mile. Then we saw him. Standing alongside the road up ahead was a slender, pale youth with long, streaming hair, his thumb beckoning us to stop.

"I've heard this one before," Retch said. "Don't stop for him!"

"We can't just let the poor devil stand out there in the rain. He'll drown," I said.

"The way the story goes," Retch said, "is that he has already . . ."

But before he could finish, I'd brought the car to a stop and the youth was crawling into the backseat. He appeared to be about eighteen, with pale eyes, pale lips, and pale hair.

We drove along in silence for some time, Retch tensely popping his knuckles and occasionally reaching back to pat down the hairs that persisted in rising on the back of his neck. Finally, I tried to strike up a bit of conversation with the lad.

"You from these parts?" I asked.

The boy said nothing.

"What were you doing out in a storm like this?"

My question was answered only by an eerie silence.

"Oh, my gosh!" Retch muttered under his breath. "I knew it. Next he's going to tell us that the bridge up ahead is washed out."

"Don't be silly," I whispered.

"The bridge up ahead is washed out," the boy said. "You'd better take the River Road to town."

I patted down a few unruly hairs on the back of my neck. "Right."

When we reached the intersection of the River Road, I stopped the car and climbed out to take a close look and make sure the road was passable. Retch scrambled out of the car with me.

"You were crazy to pick that kid up," he hissed at me. "I know he's the same one I heard about somewhere. I'm walking the rest of the way to town."

Just then a high wavering cry drifted out of the darkness up ahead.

"One thing's for sure," Retch said. "I'm not walking to town."

When we got back to the car, the pale youth was gone. We two pale, middle-aged men scrambled into the car, which spewed out twin rooster tails of mud over the boat and trailer as we shot off down the River Road.

We slid to a stop in front of the only bar in the town and bounded inside, both of us having the distinct impression that we were being trailed, possibly by a large bat. The barmaid and a scattering of patrons gave us curious stares.

"You look like you seen a ghost," the barmaid said.

"T-two double sh-shots of the st-strongest stuff you got," Retch ordered. "I don't know what he's having."

"The s-same," I said.

We then related our story to the folks in the bar. They listened with attentive solemnness, occasionally nodding as if to say, yes, yes, they knew what had happened. When we had finished, an old white-bearded fellow took off his rimless spectacles and wiped them. "I reckon you fellows have just become acquainted with the Jakes boy. He drove his car into the river a couple of years back."

"D-drove his car into the river?" Retch said.

"D-drowned?" I said.

"Drowned!" the old man said. "Heck no, he didn't drown! But driving his car into the river is apparently what give him the idea of thumbing rides on dark and stormy nights and scaring the bejeebers out of fishermen like you fellers!"

At that the regulars at the bar burst into hysterical laughter and slapped their knees black and blue and rolled around on the floor and generally gave the impression of being highly amused.

As Retch and I slunk for the door, the old man spoke again and the mirthful occupants of the room instantly suspended their hilarity. "There is one thing, though, that's a little strange about your experience. I'm kind of surprised you didn't notice it."

"What's that?" I said.

"There ain't no bridge on the highway up to the lake!"

Retch and I stomped out of the bar. If there's one thing I hate, it's a bunch of drunken yokels making a spectacle of themselves.

When we got to the car, I stared into the backseat where the Jakes boy had been sitting. "Wait a second," I said. "If that wasn't a ghost, why isn't the seat wet where he was sitting?"

Retch looked into the backseat. "You've got a point there," he said. "On the other hand, why would a ghost steal both our tackle boxes?"

The mystery was never solved, even though Retch and I spent a couple of dark and stormy nights driving up and down the highway hoping to give a lift to a lad with pale eyes, pale lips, pale hair, and two dark green tackle boxes that didn't belong to him.

The Hunters'
Workout Guide

Since prehistoric times and even earlier, hunters have engaged in strenuous physical exercises to prepare themselves for the rigors of hunting. Strangely, most hunters are still out of shape by opening day of hunting season. Why? If one discounts the tendency of hunters to start their exercise program fifteen minutes before the season opens, then it must be concluded that standard exercises are ineffective in conditioning the human body for the postures, movements, and exertions peculiar to hunting. I have, therefore, devised an exercise program especially for the hunter.

The exercises are designed to be performed in the typical business office during interruptions in the work routine, such as coffee breaks or the boss being called out of the building. This is because, as my research shows, the average hunter doesn't have time to work out at a gym. Instead, he must slave away at two or three jobs in order to pay for all the expensive paraphernalia that makes serious hunting possible—jewelry, furs, fancy dresses, and the like. Otherwise, there's no way his spouse is going to let him spend all his spare time out hunting.

Some of the exercises are intended to condition the hunter psychologically for the ordeals often encountered in the field. It is a well-known fact that a hunter's mind usually surrenders to hardship before his body, which doesn't help the mind all that much since it can't go home alone and sit by the fire with a hot toddy until the body comes stumbling in. I, on the other hand, have had occasions when the body conked out first. That's a bad one, too. My mind would say, "C'mon, there's a deer right over this next rise!" But my body would reply, "Well, go get it then, but I'm sittin' right here on this log until you get back." The trick is to have the body and mind collapse simultaneously, which is the purpose of these exercises.

Be sure to get a checkup from your doctor before undertaking the exercise program. If the doctor bursts out laughing during the exam, don't believe him when he tells you he thought of a funny joke. Just forget about getting in shape for hunting this year and take up golf instead.

Here is a test you can perform in your own home to determine your level of physical fitness. Strip off all your clothes and lie down flat on the floor. Next, push yourself up into a headstand. If you have trouble maintaining your balance, you may wish to have someone hold your feet to steady you. My research shows, by the way, that only one person in ten thousand can keep a straight face while holding the feet of a naked man who is standing on his head. Simply ignore any unseemly displays of mirth by your helper. Also, a sharp word or two spoken with authority often serves to repress the natural human urge in this situation to tickle behind the knees. It is best if you learn to stand on your head unassisted.

Now note your physical responses. If the blood pounds in your ears and behind your eyeballs and you are overcome by nausea, there is nothing to worry about. These are merely symptoms of a minor malady common in persons of middle age, which is middle age. (If you are not yet middle-aged, of course, you should start worrying.) On the other hand, if everything suddenly goes dark and you have trouble breathing, you have a serious problem—your fat has slipped down and covered your head. Persons experiencing this condition should begin the exercise program immediately.

The field situations described below are for the purpose of comparison only. You may experience greater or lesser misery depending on how and where you hunt Here, then, are the exercises.

The Ice-Breaker—For this exercise, you will need a pan of water and a large quantity of ice. Put the ice in the pan and let chill for an hour. Stick your hands in the ice water until they become totally numb. Now, jerk them out of the ice water and try to take your ballpoint pen apart and reassemble it in three seconds. This will give you the dexterity you need to reload for a quick shot during a freezing rain. Or it may give you frostbite, which is all right, too, since every hunter should be able to shoot with frostbite.

Spend your coffee breaks standing in the pan of ice water. Although your office-mates may at first think you a bit eccentric, they will soon avoid you during coffee breaks and at all other times if possible. Your concentration will thus be unbroken by idle chitchat. And it takes quite a bit of concentration to stand in a pan of ice water for fifteen minutes.

Every other day you should sit in the ice water instead of standing in it. If your supervisor asks you why you are sitting in a pan of ice water, tell him it keeps you mentally alert for the afternoon's work. Who knows, perhaps the whole office staff will be required to sit in pans of ice water during the coffee break.

To more accurately simulate the conditions of the hunt, arrange for one of your fellow workers to sneak up behind you from time to time and dump the pan of ice water down the back of your neck. The maximum conditioning will occur if, at the time, you are tired and miserable and feeling as if you can't survive for another minute.

Consistent practice of the various forms of the Ice-Breaker will prepare you for certain climatic conditions encountered on the hunt. Of course, there will be days when the weather turns bad, and nothing can prepare you for that.

The Candle—Hunters must learn to ignore pain if they are to fully enjoy their sport. A good way to condition yourself to pain is by holding your hand palm-down over a candle. Howling and dancing about during this procedure tends to detract from the desired effect of the exercise and should be avoided. Within a few weeks you should be able to hold your hand over the candle for up to five minutes without flinching. Some of your co-workers in the office may accuse you of showing off, of making a display of raw machismo. Others may openly ridicule you. Some sadist may even suggest that you use a lighted candle.

The Hindquarter Hustle—This exercise is intended to improve your upper body strength and your agility. From among your fellow workers, select one who weighs approximately one hundred pounds—about the weight of a hindquarter of an elk. Because of the size requirement, your subject will probably be a woman. Ask her if she will assist you in an exercise. Do not, I repeat, do not indicate that you have chosen her because she bears any resemblance whatsoever to the hindquarter of an elk. Then have her ride you piggyback while you step from floor to desk top, leap to a chair, step over the back of the chair and onto the floor, jump to the top of the table, down again, and finally climb up twenty-seven flights of stairs. Repeat. While this is going on, the woman should flop about and in every other way possible attempt to make you lose your balance. A word of warning: Since your employer may not be an elk hunter himself, and therefore may be incapable of comprehending the purpose of this exercise, you should perform it only when he is in a board meeting or similarly occupied.

The exercise, obviously, is intended to prepare you for the task of packing out a hindquarter of an elk you were stupid enough to shoot five miles from your vehicle in rough, steep terrain that didn't seem all that bad when you weren't packing out the hindquarter of an elk.

The Squat Walk—This exercise is sometimes referred to as the Moving Hunker. Lower yourself into the standard hunker position, with posterior no more than three or four inches above the floor. Now walk. That's all there is to it. You should try to work up to half a mile a day of the Squat Walk. Half a mile may seem rather far, but if you Squat Walk out to the water cooler or down the hall to deliver a report or out to lunch, you'll be surprised at how quickly you can do half a mile. Your fellow workers and passersby may give you odd looks and make snide remarks, but so what! Remember to keep moving, however. A stationary Squat Walk arouses suspicion, and may result in someone's calling the security people. It is very difficult to explain a stationary Squat Walk to security people.

The Squat Walk prepares you for hunting in open country where the only concealment from game is low brush. It is not unusual for hunters in this situation to Squat Walk four or five miles in a single day. Frequently, coyote hunters will Squat Run, a particularly difficult maneuver, in the direction of quavering howls wafting over the desert, only to discover the howls are coming from a Squat-Walking hunter trying to straighten up. Practicing the Squat Walk around the office will help you avoid such embarrassment.

The Five-Toe Grab—This exercise gives you the powerful toes so important to hunting. The basic technique consists of striding briskly across a room and suddenly freezing in midstride with the extended leg well forward and the foot approximately two inches above the floor. This is accomplished by gripping the floor with the toes of your other, or planted, foot. Sure it's difficult, particularly while wearing shoes, but far from impossible. Try to maintain a relaxed expression while performing this exercise, since uncontrolled grimaces have been known to rupture faces. At first, you may notice strange crackling sounds, but this is nothing more than fissures developing in your toe bones and should be ignored. After six weeks of practicing this exercise daily, you will be able to crack walnuts with your toes, though why you should want to is beyond me.

As most experienced hunters are aware, the situation for which the Five-Toe Grab prepares them is this: You are striding briskly back to your car after a day of deer hunting. The freshest tracks you have come across appear to have been made early in the last century. Deer are the furthest thing from your mind. Suddenly, as your fore boot descends toward a pile of dry twigs, you notice a nice buck standing on a knoll a mere thirty yards distant. The slightest sound will send him out of sight. You apply the Five-Toe Grab, halting the descent of your foot an inch from the twigs. While maintaining that posture, you put the crosshairs on the deer and get off your shot. This technique can be highly effective, but only on deer that are not startled by grunts that carry up to a mile on a still day.

The Desk Lift—With this exercise, you stand straddle-legged on the backs of two chairs, then bend over and pick up your office desk, after which you. . . .

But that's enough for today. I don't want you to overdo it before we get to the difficult exercises.

Temporary Measures

A full seventy-five percent of the sporting life consists of temporary measures—give or take sixty percent. Extreme cases on either end of the scale have been eliminated from the study. There was one angler, for example, who believed that if you can't do a thing right you shouldn't do it at all. A strict adherent to this philosophy, he hadn't been fishing once in the past thirty-seven years. I chastised the man for holding such a stupid belief—that there is a *right way* to fish—and told him I had a good mind to divest him of his title of angler. He told me he had a good mind to punch me in the nose. I replied that I'd like to see him try, but since I was three blocks away by then, he didn't hear me, and it's a darn good thing for him that he didn't.

Another extreme case, on the opposite end of the scale from the sorehead mentioned above, is myself. Approximately ninety-eight percent of my sporting life consists of temporary measures.

A line guide on one of my favorite fly rods is tied in place with little black mounds of sewing thread daubed with model airplane glue. As I tell anyone who notices, the mounds of thread are only a temporary measure. I intend to rewrap the rod properly as soon as I don't have something better to do. It is surprising, though, how many better things there are to do than rewrapping a rod properly. Even more surprising is that sewing thread and model airplane glue will hold a guide in place for upwards of ten years.

Someday I intend to build a decent duck blind. It will be supported by stout posts, chemically treated against rot. There will be a built-in bench inside, with a drawer underneath to hold boxes of shotgun shells. A small table will fold out from the side for lunch. I've even thought of attaching a camouflaged canvas roof that slips back automatically when I stand to shoot. For a temporary measure, though, I'll continue to stand hip-deep out in the marsh with a bunch of cattails tied around me.

As soon as I don't have something better to do, I'm going to patch that leak in the tent. Of course, rewrapping a line guide on my fly rod would be something better to do than patching a leak in a tent, so it may take a while. For a temporary measure, I sleep on the side of the tent that doesn't leak. If I have a companion along, I simply say, "Why don't you sleep on that side of the tent? It has a nice view of the stars." It also has running water, but I let him discover that for himself.

I really do want to organize my tackle box. Several years ago, I fished with a man who actually had his tackle box organized. He expressed some disapproval of my technique of hauling out a cluster of lures and spinning it around until I found the spoon that I wanted. Naturally, I was embarrassed and realized I had to do something to correct the situation. For a temporary measure, I didn't go fishing with the man anymore.

Pretty soon, when all the kids are through college, I'm going to buy myself a decent four-wheel-drive hunting rig. It will be so high off the ground I'll need a ladder to climb into it. That hunting rig will go anywhere. And there will be a nice little camper on the back, with a propane heater, comfortable beds, a refrigerator and cookstove, and a table on which my buddies and I can play cards after a hard day of fishing or hunting. Best of all, there will be a special rack up on top for hauling back the deer and elk and moose that I bag. But until I can afford the new rig, I can certainly make do with the family sedan, that's for sure. What do I care if some of the wealthier hunters get a chuckle out of my hunting rig? You'd think they had never seen a man driving home with his deer seat-belted beside him on the passenger seat.

As soon as the mortgage is paid off, I think I'll get me one of those new compound bows, the ones with all the little pulleys that enable you to hold at full stretch without trembling or without your eyeballs getting tangled in the cord. For right now, I'll have to settle for my old recurve, with its pull ranging from fifty-five to three hundred pounds, depending on how late in the day it is. As I tell my bowhunting companions, the recurve is just a temporary measure, until I get my new compound. Besides, my eyeballs need the exercise.

One of the things that has always bothered me about three-week fishing expeditions for record-busting black marlin in the South Pacific is the design of the fighting chair. After thirty minutes of fighting even a medium-sized black marlin, you can get a terrible pain in your lower back if the chair isn't just right. I want to get a custom-made fighting chair for my deep-water cruiser. For now, though, I'll get by with a boat cushion. A custom-made fighting chair would look out of place in a twelve-foot aluminum cartopper. Besides, I don't get much pain in my lower back from fighting even the big two-pound rainbows up at Trout Lake. But Trout Lake, too, is only a temporary measure, until I get enough money together for the deep-water cruiser and the three-week expeditions after black marlin in the South Pacific.

Someday I want to be able to tie size-22 flies perfectly, but until then I will have to put up with some defects. The biggest defect is that Clipper John's Fly Shop clips me $1.50 each for them. Of course, if my recurve bow continues to exercise my eyeballs, I may soon be able to see well enough to tie my own size 22s.

I've always wanted to have a good fishing companion, a man of learning and culture and good taste, a man who appreciates classical music and literature, good Scotch and fine foods, a man who knows the Latin names of flora and fauna, a man who enjoys the opportunity to commune with nature whether or not any fish are caught. Instead, my fishing companion is Retch Sweeney, who says things like, "Not one lousy fish! Don't that beat all! I wish those *bleeping* birds would shut up—they're getting on my nerves! This cheap beer ain't too bad, but it has an awful aftertaste when you belch it." Strange as it may seem, even after forty years of fishing with him, I still like to think of Retch as a temporary measure.

A friend of mind recently got himself an insulated survival suit that keeps him cozy-warm when we're out icefishing. "You ought to get one of these," he says, as the north wind comes strafing across the ice. "They keep you cozy-warm."

"Yeah, I know, that's what you keep saying," I reply. "Actually, the cold makes me feel *alive*. Say, would you mind checking my pulse to see if I still am?"

Freezing out on the ice is only a temporary measure. I fully intend to get one of those insulated suits, but I wouldn't want to give up icefishing until I do.

My sleeping bag is one of those September models. You know the kind—too hot for summer and too cold for winter, but just right for September. In fact, it's just right only for the second week of September. Unfortunately, I always have to work that week, and have never yet had the opportunity to experience the bag when it is just right. Pretty soon I'm going to buy a bag for summer and another one for winter. It seems like the only sensible thing to do. But for now, the September bag is all right, even though it's nearly July and I have to sleep with it unzipped. After all, somebody has to take care of feeding the carnivorous insects.

My wife points out that if I didn't spend so much time out hunting and fishing and "cavorting about in the wilds," I would have time to earn more money and then I could buy all the stuff I need to do things properly, and I wouldn't have to put up with so many temporary measures. But I have an even better solution. If you just leave temporary measures alone long enough, they eventually become permanent measures. Then you don't have to take any time away from your hunting and fishing and cavorting about in the wilds to earn a bunch of money. I've been aging some of my temporary measures for over thirty years now and, if my guess is right, several of them are just about ready to turn permanent.

The Fibricators

Young Elwood Fitch stopped by the house the other day to tell me he had caught a five-pound cutthroat under the bridge on Sand Creek. He said he had taken the fish on a No. 16 Black Gnat he had tied himself. Elwood is only twelve, but even so I couldn't help but be disappointed in him.

"Elwood," I said, "you don't expect me to believe a fish story like that, do you?"

Embarrassed, the lad hung his head and scuffed some shag off my carpet with the toe of his boot. "I sorta hoped you would."

"Not a chance," I said. "Now, tell me the truth."

Elwood confessed that actually the fish was a perch that weighed considerably less than half a pound and he had caught it in Bott's Lake on a night crawler his little brother had sold to him for a nickel.

I shook my head. "Elwood, don't you know that

when you tell fishing lies the way you just did you tarnish the credibility of all the rest of us anglers?"

"I'm sorry," he said.

"All right, everybody makes mistakes," I said. "But I want you to promise me one thing."

"What's that?"

"That you'll learn how to tell fishing lies properly. No self-respecting angler would believe a fish story the way you told that one. Pull up a chair and I'll give you a few pointers."

As I told Elwood, I have been a student of fibrication most of my life. In fact, I remember the very first story I ever fibricated.

I was about six years old and had stopped by the cabin of an old couple who lived back in the woods near our farm. Homer and Emma seemed delighted by my visit and invited me in for a glass of lemonade. After we were seated comfortably around their table, the old man leaned over and asked me, "Well, young man, what's the news?"

News? There was no news that I was aware of, but my hosts were looking at me with expressions of such eager anticipation that I didn't feel I should disappoint them.

"Just the bus wreck," I said.

The two old people snapped upright. "What'd he say, Emma?" the old man shouted.

"He said there was a bus wreck!" Emma shouted back.

I hadn't expected my small contribution to the conversation to arouse such excitement, but was pleased to have interrupted the day's tedium for the old folks with a bit of "news." I thought they would be satisfied with just the headline, but they weren't. They pressed me for details.

"When did it happen?" Emma asked me. "We haven't heard anything about a bus wreck."

"About a half hour ago," I said, for no particular reason other than a vague notion that news should be as fresh as possible.

"Good lord!" cried Homer. "Where?"

"Why, down at the big bend in the highway near our place."

Never before had my efforts at small talk aroused such interest and enthusiasm in adults. Homer and Emma bounded to their feet, danced around the table, knocked over chairs, stepped on assorted dogs and cats, and shouted questions at me so fast my head began to heat up from the strain of concocting new and frightful details.

"Anybody killed?" cried Homer.

I took a long drag on the lemonade and wiped my mouth on my sleeve. "Fifteen people," I said.

Not having any great experience with numbers, I had selected fifteen more or less at random. From the way Homer's and Emma's jaws sagged, I knew I had picked a good number, one the old couple held in high esteem.

"Most of them women and children," I added, shaking my head for dramatic effect and to give emphasis to the sheer awfulness of the disaster.

While I was pondering the possibility of having an airplane crash into the bus, the old couple scooped up towels, sheets, and blankets, and before I knew what was happening, they had loped off in the direction of the accident, apparently with the idea of offering aid and comfort to the survivors, if any.

Amid an uproar of dogs and cats, I sat alone at the table, nervously sipping my lemonade, happy to have brought a note of excitement into the lives of Homer and Emma, but fighting off the ominous feeling that I was not yet finished with The Great Bus Wreck, as it was to be henceforth known. After hiding out in the woods for most of the day, I was finally driven home by threat of darkness. My sister, The Troll, was waiting for me on the back porch. She turned and called out happily to my mother, "Hey, Ma, Walter Winchell finally got home! Do you want me to bring the stick?" Even in those days the news business was filled with stress.

Technically, The Great Bus Wreck fib doesn't qualify as a fish story, because a fish wasn't included among the ingredients. It does, however, contain the essentials of proper form: an attitude of casual disinterest on the part of the fibricator, a gradual compounding of the magnitude of the event being fibricated, and the insertion of a variety of specific details. I was a natural fibricator. Still, at the age of six, I lacked the necessary craft and polish to "take in" experienced anglers with one of my fish stories.

A few years later, much to my good fortune, I became acquainted with Rancid Crabtree, who had devoted his whole life to mastery of the art of fibrication. Rancid was the Picasso of the fib. He could do little white fibs, big blue fibs, realistic fibs, impressionistic fibs, expressionistic fibs, abstract fibs, surrealistic fibs, nonobjective fibs, and even pop fibs. As with any genius, Rancid extended the limits of the art far beyond anything that had been known before. Fibrication was an all-consuming activity to him. In the years I knew him, I don't think I caught him in more than half a dozen truths, and each of those so minuscule as to be unnoteworthy except for its rarity, like, say, a one-legged woodpecker.

Rancid tended to be a purist, and most of his fibs were created primarily as fibs for fibs' sake. On the other hand, he never hesitated to manufacture a functional fib whenever an occasion arose.

One time Rancid and I were just returning to the road from one of our secret fishing spots when we ran into three characters whom Rancid regarded as unsavory, which is to say that they were known to engage in activities the old woodsman despised—regular jobs. The trio consisted of the town barber, dentist, and undertaker, and two guys who worked at the sawmill. They gawked at our string of plump trout and then took some sightings along the corridor we had just carved through the thick brush that concealed a lovely set of beaver dams a quarter mile distant. Scarcely taking time to grunt greetings at us, the men extracted their fly rods from an automobile and began to assemble them.

"What'd you take them fish on?" one of the men asked.

"Got any pickled sow's yars with ya?" Rancid asked. "Thet's the only thang these fish'll bite on."

"Yars?" the man said.

"Pickled sow's ears," I translated.

"No, we ain't got any of them," one of the other fellows put in, "but we got some mighty fine flies."

"Wall, good luck to ya," Rancid said, starting to walk away. Then he stopped and turned and said, "Say, iffin you fellers see maw big black dog, Wuff, would you mind haulin' him back to town? He can find his way home from thar."

"Oh, I reckon," a man said without any great show of enthusiasm.

"I'd be beholdin' to ya," Rancid said. "Course, if

Wuff be all tore up when ya find him, jist put him out of his misery."

"Tore up?" another man said.

"Yep. I 'spect thet big cat might of kilt him outright, but mebby not."

"Big cat?"

"Jist an ol' mountin' lion. But don't worry none, cause they almost never attacks a hoomin bean lessen they's hurt an' starvin'."

The three men faltered in the assembly of their rods.

"Come to thank of it," Rancid continued in a musing manner, "thet ol' cat did seem a bit on the thin side, didn't you thank so, boy?"

"You could count his ribs," I said.

Rancid raised an eyebrow at me in an expression that said, "That ain't bad." By now the men were taking down their rods, so Rancid and I ambled off up the road.

"Hope you find your dog," one of the men called after us, apparently thankful we had saved him from being torn to bits.

"Oh yeah, me too," Rancid said. "Ol' Rex, he was a purty good ol' dog."

"Wuff," I corrected, but the three men were too distracted to pay attention to minor discrepancies.

"Shucks," Rancid said later. "Ah didn't even git to use the part about the quicksand."

"Or the poisonous ticks," I said.

"Yeah," Rancid said. "The pisonous ticks. Ain't nobody yet gone up agin the pisonous ticks!"

That's your basic functional fib. But Rancid used the functional fib only in emergencies. His preference, as I said, was for the pure fib, the fib for fib's sake. I think the motive behind Rancid's fibrication was his belief that ordinary life was insufficient and required enhancement. I'd spend a wet, cold, dull day out in the woods with Rancid and my general impression of the experience was that it had been wet and cold and dull. But later, upon hearing Rancid tell someone about the day, I would discover that it had been full of wild adventures and startling occurrences and rare spectacles. Afterward, I always remembered Rancid's version of the day rather than my own impression of it, because Rancid's was so much more interesting and entertaining and even magical. Reality always played second fiddle to Rancid's imagination.

At the close of my lecture, I could see that young Elwood was fairly bursting with a question. It is a wonderful thing to see intellectual curiosity suddenly take flower in youth.

"Yes, Elwood, what is it?"

"You got any good junk food in the house?"

"No, you little toad, I don't believe in junk food! You can have some celery or carrot sticks if you like."

"Naw. Well, I'd better be going. See ya."

After he left, I worried about how Elwood would survive modern life with no more understanding of fibrication than he has. Indeed, such was my anxiety over poor Elwood that I wandered out to the kitchen and absent-mindedly consumed a whole package of Yummy Yum-Yums, half a leftover pizza, and two cans of cream soda.

The Family
Camper's Dictionary

Every year thousands of Americans are introduced to the sport of camping. (Many of them are wives and mothers who don't want the meeting to occur in the first place, but no matter.) To ease their transition from the comforts of home to life in the wilds, I have compiled the following dictionary of terms, phrases, yelps, howls, and miscellaneous weird sounds.

Camping itself is a rather vague term. For example, the infliction of the average family camping trip on prisoners of war would be considered a violation of the Geneva Convention. On the other hand, it is considered perfectly all right, and even *fun,* for a father and mother and their young children to subject themselves to the same experience. When it comes to camping, cruel and unusual punishment is in the eye of the beholder, along with smoke from the campfire.

This is not to say that family camping trips are free of protest. Generally, the protest occurs in the middle of a stormy night while the family bobs about on air mattresses in the flooded tent. One of the common forms of protest is: "You just try to pull something like this again, George, and I'm consulting a divorce lawyer!"

There are many kinds of camping. *Car camping,* for example, is where the camp is within twenty feet of the car, and a portion of each night is actually spent in the car, either because the tent collapsed or somebody thought he "heard a bear."

Backpacking is where the camp is located more than twenty feet from the car, and no portion of the night is spent actually in the car, except in the case of dire emergencies, such as when somebody thinks he "saw a bear."

Solitary camping is where a lone camper lies awake all night wondering how he could have been so stupid as not to have brought somebody along to camp with him. You know you are involved in solitary camping when you ask "Did you hear that funny sound just then?" and nobody answers. Of course it may be that the reason you are suddenly involved in solitary camping is that the person you were with heard that funny sound just then and is now engaged in car camping.

Group camping may consist of as many as forty individuals, none of whom thought to bring a can opener. A Cub Scout outing is typical of group camping, and it often ends with the adult leader spending the night pressed inside a pup tent with fourteen Cub Scouts because somebody had the bright idea of telling scary stories around the campfire.

Roughing-it camping is where the camp is so basic as to be devoid of even hot showers.

There are many other forms of camping, but they are mostly combinations or variations of the above or with no relation to them at all. Let us, therefore, proceed to the Family Camper's Dictionary:

Corn flakes—A common camp food. Often eaten dry with salt and pepper since no one thought to bring milk.

Hominy—Whenever there is a camping disaster, the only food saved.

"Looks like we may be stranded here for a week," a camper says. "Did we save any of the food?"

"Just the fifteen cans of hominy," he is told, which scarcely seems worth the trouble of surviving.

Oddly enough, the only food saved is never the canned beef stew. Cans of beets, parsnips, or squash may turn up as substitutes for the hominy. The mysterious thing is that nobody can ever remember seeing any of these foods in the grub box prior to the disaster.

The aroma of frying bacon—What campers love to wake up to.

As my wife and I climbed into our sleeping bags one evening a while back, I told her, "You know what I love to wake up to on camping trips, Bun? The aroma of frying bacon."

"Oh, yeah?" she said. "Well, I'll have to see if I can find it in a spray can next time I'm in the store."

If you're unlucky enough to have an insensitive and stubborn spouse, you may go through many years of camping without waking up to the aroma of frying bacon.

"Something hairy just ran across my neck!"—An announcement made by a young child immediately after the lantern has been shut off in the tent. Once the screaming from the other children has died down, the parents explain to the kid that it was just his imagination. Then for the rest of the night the parents experience the sensation of hairy things running across their necks

NEVER SNIFF A GIFT FISH

Cloudburst—A natural phenomenon that, when it occurs in the middle of the night, reminds a young child that he forgot to go to the bathroom before turning in after being told to do so nine times.

A big black stump—What the young child thinks is a bear while he is going to the bathroom in the middle of the night during a cloudburst, and which his father, peering through the rain and urging the child to act with expediency, also thinks is a bear.

A bear—What is thought to produce any night sound within a mile radius of the campsite. Also, what is standing on your picnic table munching your camp cooler when you stroll out of the tent, saying to the children, "See, Daddy isn't afraid. He knows it is just a little chip—!"

Yip-yip-yip-Owoooooo!—The haunting, melodic call of coyotes singing to each other in the hills. Also, the spine-tingling cry of a camper trying to pound in a tent peg with a rock.

Camping manuals—Books filled with ingenious camping tips which are forgotten the instant the camper sets foot in the field. "I read about a way to cook a chicken with a camera lens and a wire clothes hanger, but I can't remember how," he says. "Better just fry it."

Wire clothes hangers—The most useful camping tools ever invented. May be used for roasting meat over a fire, holding cooking pots, lashing tent poles together, and many other services. Once, I even saw a camper hang his clothes on one.

S'Mores—Child's standard camping dessert, consisting of chocolate bars and toasted marshmallows sandwiched between graham crackers. Have been known to cause child to become semipermanently attached to his clothes, sleeping bag, pine needles, and anything else he comes in contact with. Although a child may consume half a dozen S'Mores, two are considered a lethal dose for adults.

Unimproved Forest Service Campground—A designation on Forest Service maps to indicate a small swamp used for experimental breeding of killer mosquitoes.

New binoculars—What one of your children vaguely remembers having last seen when he set them on a log during a rest stop earlier in the day. *New camera* may be substituted for *new binoculars*.

"What do you mean, get up? It's still dark out!"— What your youngest child says upon awakening upside down in his sleeping bag.

Pants pockets—Containers to which young campers eventually transfer the entire contents of their packs.

Suspenders—What the young camper needs to hold up his pants pockets. Not unusual for a kid's suspenders to shoot him out of camp when he dumps his pockets.

"When hell freezes over"—An expression used by wives and mothers to indicate the next time you'll get them to go on another camping trip.

"A nice hot bath"—An odd phrase that wives and mothers insert into every other sentence after the second day of a camping trip.

A toasted marshmallow—What a kid calls the flaming projectile he lobs at your lap from the end of a sharpened willow.

Call of the wild—Sound made by parents as they search the woods for a kid who is asleep in the back of the station wagon.

Downwind—Whichever side of the campfire you happen to be on.

Bicycle campers—Hearty individuals who walk about camp with a pained expression on their bodies.

Cowboy coffee—A beverage made by throwing a handful of coffee in boiling water, and which causes your legs to bow when you take a sip of it.

"Come and get it!"—Plea telephoned to tow truck company by camper who was dumb enough to back his car into an Unimproved Forest Service Campground.

A roasted wiener—What your wife says you look like after you have spent a July day hiking shirtless in shorts.

Squirrel—Guy in neighboring campsite who plays transistor radio at full volume most of the night.

Gorp—A mix of fruits and nuts. Also, a derogatory term applied to the rowdy group in the next campsite.

Eye-opener—Early-morning shot of cowboy coffee. Also, loud snuffling sound just outside the tent.

Woodcraft—Sneaky tactic used to fool your spouse into getting up and building the morning fire.

Last beer—The one you forgot you drank *before* you took the kids on a hike to the top of the mountain.

National Park Campground—What all the campers came here to get away from.

Bug bite—What the camper tries to avoid taking while he is eating outside in an Unimproved Forest Service Campground.

Grill—The questioning of a child who vaguely remembers having set your new binoculars on a log a few rest stops back.

Granny knot—What you feel like after spending a night sleeping with your spouse and three children in a pup tent.

"I'll hold my breath"—Childish threat made to keep from eating the special stew you've prepared for supper. Tell her if she doesn't eat it she'll be setting a bad example for the children.

Camp dump—The back seat of your car on the way home.

"Don't tell me it's over already"—Sarcasm used by wives and mothers at the termination of camping trips.

"Who's going to help me wash all this stuff and put it away?"—An indication that it's not over already.

The Big Match

The long-distance phone call from my nephew and fishing manager, Dr. Mike Gass, was typical of him—warm, witty, and with the charges reversed.

"Hey, Unc, I got a great match arranged for you," Mike shouted over the phone. "This guy is a top contender."

"Sounds good," I said. "Who is it?"

"Tuck Harry."

"Not *the* Tuck Harry," I gasped. "Listen, Mike, maybe you'd better call the match off. I've been slowing down a lot lately, and my reflexes aren't what they used to be. Tuck Harry may just be too good for me."

"Come on, Unc, don't try to kid me," Mike said jovially. "You haven't been beaten yet, have you?"

That was true. I had defended my title dozens of times against some of the top contenders in the sport and always emerged victorious. You see, I am the World

210

Champion of not-catching fish and not-shooting game. Oh, for recreation and relaxation, I will occasionally catch a fish or shoot a grouse or pheasant. Indeed, as a youngster I was never without a fishing rod or shotgun in hand, which was awkward at church and while taking baths, but otherwise a great way of life. My skill at hunting and fishing was surpassed only by an abundance of luck, and I had no trouble keeping the family table well supplied with fish and game.

Alas, tragedy brought to an abrupt end my carefree and happy life. At the tender age of twenty-five, I was struck down by the necessity of having to take a regular job. As a result of this catastrophe, my hunting and fishing were limited to weekends and sick leave, the latter so frequent that my boss would have fired me if he hadn't thought I was terminally ill and would be leaving soon anyway.

As the amount of time I could spend in the outdoors diminished, so did my skills and luck. My hunting and fishing friends began to feel sorry for me and took to arranging special little outings to their secret places.

"Listen," one of them would say, "I guarantee you will catch fish where I'm taking you." We'd go there and I wouldn't catch any fish. "All right," the fellow would say. "Now I mean business. I'm taking you to a spot I've never even told anybody else about. You must swear never to tell where you caught the fish." We'd go there and I wouldn't get a strike.

Hunting was no different. A pitying friend would tell me, "This time you're going to get your deer for certain. I've got this secret place staked out, with a deer practically tied to a tree for you. You won't be able to miss." And I wouldn't miss. I wouldn't even get to shoot.

At best, we'd find some stale tracks in the secret place, indicating that a deer had passed earlier in the century.

I concealed my disappointment over these failures by the ruse of gnashing my teeth and kicking trees. Reflecting upon the phenomenon, however, it occurred to me that not only didn't I catch fish or shoot game on the outings, neither did anyone in my party. I began to think that perhaps I had some peculiar psychic power that nullified the rhythms of the natural world. It was as though a magnetic field radiated out from me and affected even my companions. Unfortunately, my companions came to a similar conclusion. Soon I couldn't suggest a hunting or fishing trip to them without it conflicting with one of their "previous engagements" on that date, which was odd, since most of these guys usually didn't even know the months of the year. All they knew were the seasons—trout season, grouse season, deer season, etc.

It is the nature of the true sportsman, however, to seek out a challenge. If the taking of fish or game becomes too easy, he soon tires of it, and begins looking for ways to make the sport more difficult for himself and to improve the odds for the quarry. The angler, for example, will go from hooks baited with worms to wet flies to dry flies so tiny that they look as if they've been tied under an electronic microscope. His fly rods will become increasingly lighter until they are all but invisible. I've seen fly fishers using rods so light I didn't know if they were casting or trying to catch gnats in the air with their bare hand. My friend Orvis Fenwick once made half a dozen casts before he realized he hadn't picked up his rod.

Thus it was that the master hunters and anglers in

our area began to look upon me as the ultimate challenge. "Catching any fish lately?" one of these master sportsmen would be asked. "No, I haven't had a strike all summer," would come the answer. "But I fish exclusively with McManus, you know." An expression of awe would come over the questioner's face. "Gee," he would say admiringly. "I would like to work up to that some day."

Eventually, word spread about my prowess at not-catching fish and not-shooting game, and fishing and hunting guides from around the country began sending me invitations to go a few rounds with them. They knew that if they could induce me to catch fish or shoot game, their reputations would be made. I skunked them all. Some of them even gave up halfway through the bout, complaining of stomach cramps.

So many invitations were arriving, I finally asked my nephew Mike to become my manager, and to take over the business of arranging matches.

"I've got a great idea," he told me. "How about this? You start out by catching a few fish, see, and then we make a bet with the guide that you won't catch any more fish. We'll clean up!"

"Sounds good to me," I said. "But how do I catch the first few fish?"

"Yeah, I suppose that might be a problem, given your past record."

We decided to scrap the idea of my becoming a not-catching-fish hustler.

Even so, I have been banned from several states. When I went hunting in Montana a few years ago, no one in the state got so much as a shot the ten days I was there. It was an outstanding display of power on my part, but now the only way I can get into Montana during the hunting season is by wearing my Truman Capote disguise. This explains why several Montanans have reported seeing Capote gnash his teeth and kick trees because he missed an elk—missed it by at least three weeks, if the condition of the tracks was any sort of indication.

Members of outdoor clubs in Idaho take turns patrolling the borders in an effort to keep me out of the state, but I can usually manage to elude them. To punish them, I frequently extend my stay in the state well after I've become bored with not-catching fish and not-shooting game.

Steelheaders in Oregon, I understand, have put a bounty on me, and will pay it to anyone who brings in my license and steelhead card. This seems a bit extreme, since I shut off the fishing in Oregon only a dozen or so times a year. Furthermore, I have it on reliable testimony that the instant I leave the state, the steelheading becomes fantastic and remains so for some weeks afterward.

But now I was worried about the match that Mike had arranged for me with Tuck Harry. Tuck is a young fishing guide who works the rivers of western Washington state. He has built up a formidable reputation for helping his clients connect with steelhead. He would be tough to beat. Still, I had left some of the best and toughest fishing guides in the country sobbing into their bait buckets.

The reason I was worried is that, fishing alone the previous week, I had caught three nice trout. Naturally, I hadn't told anyone about the catch, except my wife, whom I revived by rubbing an ice cube on her forehead. Then there was the close call last summer, when I was stream fishing. A monstrous trout had made a pass at my Renegade, and I saved the day only by snapping the fly away from its jaws and integrating thirty feet of line with a thorn apple immediately to my rear. It had been close. I was haunted by the thought that maybe my luck was about to go good.

In the grim light of a cold and foggy dawn, Mike and I met Tuck Harry on the bank of a river, the name and location of which I was sworn not to divulge. The local steelheaders are more secretive than the Mafia. It is rumored that if one of the members reveals the fantastic fishing in the river to an outsider, one of the other steelheaders will grab him and kiss him on both cheeks. Strangely, this does not often prove fatal, although the victim will have recurring fits of nausea for the next five years.

I quickly sized up Tuck, as Mike and I watched him wrestle the drift boat from the trailer and, grunting and gasping, drag it to the river. We would have helped him, but long experience has taught me that this kind of exertion takes a lot out of a guide, particularly with Mike and me in the boat. Nevertheless, the young man retained an air of confidence and seemed in complete control of the situation. I found this disconcerting and began to wonder if I was not in over my head. As it turned out, I was in only up to my armpits, having inadvertently stepped backward out of the boat.

"Thatta way to go," Mike whispered to me as I changed into dry clothes. "That staggered Tuck, and it's only the first round!"

Tuck recovered quickly, however, and no sooner had we shoved off than he retaliated by drifting the boat through a wild stretch of whitewater. Cleverly, Mike and

I concealed our anxiety from the guide by reciting the Twenty-third Psalm in unison.

Tuck pulled up across from one of his secret holes and rigged me an outfit. "Keep your thumb lightly on the spool of the reel when you cast," he explained, since I had told him most of my experience in recent years had been with spinning rather than with bait-casting reels.

"That's it, you've nearly got it," Tuck said encouragingly, after my first attempted cast. "Now, let me get my knife and I'll have your thumb freed from that backlash in no time."

"Actually," I replied casually, "I'd just as soon you freed my elbow and left foot first, if you don't mind."

I soon mastered the bait-casting reel with a few practice casts. Then Tuck instructed me to cast up to the head of the hole, take up the slack quickly, and allow the sinker to bounce along the bottom of the river. "They're in there," he said of the steelhead. "You should get a strike."

His confidence in my hooking a steelhead was unnerving. I countered immediately by fastening hook, line, and sinker irretrievably to some rocks on the riverbed, a technique that proved so effective I repeated it a dozen times during the next hour. Then I switched to snagging limbs, logs, and curious livestock that watched us drift by. By noon, Tuck was on the ropes.

The fear that my luck might be turning good proved unfounded. In two days of drifting down the river from dawn to dark, I got not a single strike. Furthermore, neither did Mike nor Tuck. Nor did the hundred or so other steelheaders on the river. Some of the latter, recognizing me and knowing of my reputation, shook their fists and yelled at Tuck, "Get him out of here!" It was, if I do say so myself, one of my most inspired performances.

I felt sorry for Tuck, of course, since he had put up a fine scrap and shown good sportsmanship and didn't gnash his teeth and kick trees, as do some guides. That's why I was so happy to hear that, the day after I left, everyone in Tuck's boat took limits of steelhead, and the other steelheaders reported that it was the best day of fishing they had ever seen on the river. It's hard for me to control my elation over news like that.